——Inviting the Wolf In——

—— Inviting the Wolf In ——
Thinking About the Difficult Story

Loren Niemi & Elizabeth Ellis

August House Publishers, Inc.
LITTLE ROCK

For those who cannot speak
and must be heard

Published 2001 by August House Publishers, Inc.
P.O. Box 3223, Little Rock, Arkansas, 72203, 501-372-5450.

Printed in the United States of America

10 9 8 7 6 5 4 3 2 1   HB
10 9 8 7 6 5 4 3 2 1   PB

LIBRARY OF CONGRESS CATALOGING-IN-PUBLICATION DATA

Niemi, Loren, 1947–
  Inviting the wolf in : thinking about the difficult story /
Loren Niemi & Elizabeth Ellis.
      p. cm.
  Includes bibliographical references.
  ISBN 0-87483-656-5 (hardback : alk. paper)—
  ISBN 0-87483-623-9 (pbk.: alk. paper)
  1. Storytelling—Psychological aspects. 2. Folklore—Psychological aspects.
  3. Psychoanalysis and folklore. 4. Symbolism in folklore.
  I. Ellis, Elizabeth, 1943– II. Title.
GR72.3 .N54 2001
808.5'43'019—dc21   2001002825

Executive editor: Liz Parkhurst
Cover and book design: Joy Freeman
Cover art: Beth Stover

The paper used in this publication meets the minimum requirements
of the American National Standard for Information Sciences-
Permanence of Paper for Printed Library Materials, ANSI Z39.48-1984.

AUGUST HOUSE   PUBLISHERS   LITTLE ROCK

CONTENTS

7 INTRODUCTION: What Is a "Difficult Story"?

   8 Who Benefits from a Storytelling Approach to the Telling of Difficult Stories?

  15 What We Are and What We Are Not

19 ONE: The Need to Shape and Artfully Tell the Difficult Story

  24 STORY: "By the Grace of God," Loren Niemi

  32 The Value of Speaking Truthfully

  33 Personal Meaning and Shared Meaning

  35 STORY: "Demeter and Persephone, 1984," Elizabeth Ellis

  40 The Value of Speaking Artfully

  41 STORY: "Mitterand's Last Meal," Loren Niemi

47 TWO: Self-Censorship

55 THREE: A Consideration of Some Basic Principles

  56 Trust

  58 Permission

  59 Ownership

61 FOUR: Traditional Stories

  63 STORY: "Mister Fox," Elizabeth Ellis

  70 The Gift and Shadow of "Modern" Retellings

  71 STORY: "Hansel and Gretel," Loren Niemi

79 FIVE: Historical Stories

    83 STORY: "Mary McLeod Bethune," Elizabeth Ellis

    88 -isms of All Kinds

91 SIX: Emotional Timelines

    92 Jealousy

    94 STORY: "Just Perfect," Elizabeth Ellis

    99 STORY: "Seeing Miss Julie," Loren Niemi

    104 Grief

    106 STORY: "Thom's Dream," Megan Wells

115 SEVEN: Structural Elements Used in the Creation of Stories

    116 Tone

    119 Point of View

    121 STORY: "Hannah on a Summer's Day," Loren Niemi

    126 Point of Entry

131 EIGHT: A Wickedness-Loss Continuum

    132 The Continuum as Story Tree

    139 The Seed Story

    142 Examples of Wickedness

    148 Examples of Loss

157 NINE: Overarching Structural Elements

    158 Emotional Arc

    160 STORY: "Slaughter House," Tim Herwig

    166 Moral Framework

    167 STORY: "The Rug," Loren Niemi

    172 STORY: "Political Prisoner," Elizabeth Ellis

183 TEN: Confidentiality, Community, and Practice

187 BIBLIOGRAPHY: Difficult Stories and Spirituality

What Is a "Difficult Story"?

The world is so full of care and sorrow that it is a gracious
debt we owe to one another to discover the bright crystals of
delight hidden in somber circumstances and irksome tasks.
                                        —Helen Keller

A difficult story is any story whose content makes it challenging
to tell or uncomfortable to hear.

Frankly, almost any story can be difficult to tell. What makes
this especially so is the realization that stories are as personal as
fingerprints and as mutable as mercury. They are also potentially
as toxic as mercury if the story is not understood by the teller—
or is told to the wrong audience in the wrong context or for the
wrong reason.

What makes a story difficult changes with those who hear it
and the context in which it is heard. A story that might be
thought quite tame as part of a theater presentation could be a
difficult story if told at the Rotary Club. Not that those who
attend the Rotary Club may not also attend the theater, but
rather that they are unaccustomed to emotionally challenging
material at the club meeting. Material that might be thought of
as very entertaining in a concert setting might be thought too
edgy for church. The stories of faith and deeply held spiritual

beliefs that draw people to attend church may—when presented in a secular setting—make some listeners suspicious of the teller's intent or hostile to the message of the story.

A given story may be difficult for the listener or it may be personally problematic. A story may be difficult for the teller to present because it deals with an emotionally charged topic. It may speak to their sense of shame or be potentially embarrassing. What might have been easy to tell in one context may become difficult in another in the face of traumatic change, such as the experience of death or divorce. These events are often unsettling. By turning our personal world upside down, they may shift how we see and speak of the events in our life.

The telling of a difficult story is a revelation of self. If you have not thought about the why and how of it, you may reveal more than is intended.

Who Benefits from a Storytelling Approach —to the Telling of Difficult Stories?

In writing this book, Elizabeth and Loren begin with the fundamental assumption that it is essential and beneficial to tell difficult stories, the stories of wickedness and loss, sorrow and grief. Difficulty is inevitable. We cannot avoid hardship, pain, and tragedy in our lives. People have accidents, suffer failures and setbacks, get sick, die. Likewise, we make mistakes, suffer lapses in judgment, let the selfish and needy part of our nature lead us to doing foolish or wicked things. It is part and parcel of living.

The question is: how do we understand the meaning of these events? From our perspective there is no value in stopping our ears and stilling our tongues. Such actions will not make tragedy, bad judgment, or abuse go away. Indeed, often the first step in ending suffering is to name it for what it is, to bring it to light that others may understand what has happened. In order to take ction, we must understand that there is a need to end the statu quo.

This book sprang from a simple question: how can v learn from our troubles and how can we share those experienc with others in a way that helps them learn and grow?

The answer to that question is also a simple one: tell the story. We believe that to understand, shape, and honestly tell the difficult story is to touch the core of what it means to be human.

We will go into some detail about the meaning of that statement later, but the reality is human beings have a deep-seated need to make sense of our lives. Story is the best mechanism to fulfill that need.

Those who can benefit for the focus of this book include:

Storytellers (oral and written)

One of the highest compliments you can offer an artist in our culture is to say that he or she is a storyteller. We apply the term to writers, television and filmmakers, playwrights, even dancers and painters. What is usually meant by the compliment is that the artist's work not only has a narrative quality, but it invites audiences into the narrative.

If the role of the storyteller is to entertain, educate, and enchant, we believe that a careful consideration of the difficult story can help the artist achieve those ends. When we say *storyteller*, we refer to both the traditional spoken (oral) word and the written word. All references to storytellers and storytelling in this book are to both oral and written processes of consciously shaping language to share a story with an audience.

In our role as artists and keepers of cultural memory, we often have to tell difficult stories. This is true whether we are telling stories from our own experience or others', whether from the seat of imagination or memory. Often it is the difficult story that engages the audience and provides the lessons of great heroism or villainy. From David facing Goliath to the killing fields of Cambodia; from Arthur pulling the sword from the stone to Neil Armstrong setting foot on the moon, stories of survival and triumph invite the audience to reflect on what it means to be human.

Few have done it better than Shakespeare. *Macbeth, King Lear, Romeo and Juliet,* even *A Midsummer Night's Dream* are at their core stories about the price and meaning of our humanity via power, pride, love, and pretense. Not every artist is as successful as the Bard in crafting the difficult story. In what follows, we will present some ways for any artist to think about difficult stories. Like Shakespeare and other great voices of the human heart, we can recognize and begin to shape the difficult stories that we have longed to—or been afraid to—tell.

Shakespeare found the balance between entertainment and revelation in the telling of troubling stories. We are concerned with identifying ways to think about our experience and tell the hard truth of the matter. Like Shakespeare, we wish to find the balance between that which satisfies and that which makes us wonder and reflect while telling our troubling tales. How can we let the hard truth be heard? Where can we enable our listeners to understand that this could just as easily happen to them, even as they are wishing that it would never happen to anyone?

In the midst of his most tragic tales, Shakespeare introduced such characters as the "grave robbers" to provide comic relief. Their presence breaks the tension and allows us to release our most troubling feelings. It is often in the release of laughter that education occurs. In that moment, our guard is down. The seed of learning about how we respond to the foibles of being human can be successfully planted.

Therapists

What is therapy if not a guided process of thinking about what it means to be human, what it is to face difficulty, and what it is to change? Therapists of every stripe listen to difficult stories all the time. What can they learn from this book, especially since we make no claim to being therapists ourselves?

As storytellers, we understand that there is an essential value in speaking and being heard. We see it in every audience we tell stories to. People want to share an understanding of what it means to live, to have their experience validated, whether through metaphor or through personal narrative. In story we invite listeners inside the experience of how, why, and what if.

Inside the most common stories we tell at the water cooler or over the kitchen table are core images that are essentially metaphoric and mythological at their base. The image of the "wicked stepmother" or "King Midas" carry meanings that are shared and often unquestioned. In the process of thinking about the difficult story, we will also examine the power of images to carry this kind of added meaning and reside in our collective memory.

As often as we satisfy the need for intimacy in a story, we recognize that people want to speak their own truth. For therapists, thinking about how the difficult story can be shaped helps them hear the client's story. Knowing how to tell it may also help them respond to the client's need to speak and be heard.

We believe there is a value in therapists being able to recognize and use metaphoric stories. Sigmund Freud knew this. So did Carl Jung. Often the most direct path to understanding is not a straight line, but the journey into imagination. We often speak of dreams as riddles, personal narratives colored with the imagery of witches and giants, caves and treasure chests. We draw our lessons by analogy, using symbols and metaphors to speak from one portion of the self to another. By the illustration of behavior and values in the context of parables, fables, folktales, and myths, we can get to what lies at the core of living. In those indirect stories, the cumulative learning of generations is passed on.

Ministers

In a culture of "should" and "ought," it is often difficult to arrive at understanding and forgiveness. We often profess, as they say, to hate the sin but love the sinner. It would be much easier to love the sinner if we could understand that we have more in common with him than not. This book can be a valuable tool for ministers in thinking about their approach to hearing and telling difficult stories. The process we utilize can be helpful in building better models of understanding, compassion, and forgiveness.

We also believe there is a value in rethinking traditional religious texts. While many ministers are good about interpreting the meaning of parables in a theological context, we think that by applying our recommended principles and techniques to those texts you can tell those stories in a new way—in effect, putting new flesh on dry bones. Whether you do so as an omniscient narrator or as active participant, for religious texts to be engaging it is helpful to tell them as vital and inviting tales. Whether you recast the old stories in a modern context or reverently enter the sacred texts, by using the techniques in this book, you allow their troubling and inspiring qualities to be manifest for your listeners to experience their continuing relevance to our everyday lives.

Teachers

Teachers often complain that they are asked to wear too many hats, that there is an expectation that they will be all things to all students. Our consideration of difficult stories can provide some practical tools for classroom problem identification and solving. By developing skills in listening to—and telling—difficult stories, teachers can improve their ability to communicate to *and for* those who cannot tell their own stories.

One of the benefits of using storytelling in the classroom is building community with students. Moreover, creating safe spaces in which students can speak their experience can also foster a community of compassion in which differences and hurts can be understood and brought to light. There is no way to do that without having to hear and respond to difficult stories.

Community Workers and Human Service Professionals

Loren has spent a good portion of his life working as a community organizer in urban neighborhoods. He knows from direct experience that storytelling offers many benefits to those on the forefront of social change and community development. Understanding the way in which difficult stories are shaped and told provides a metaphoric canary in the coal mine, a way of tracking dysfunction from the individual to the family to the neighborhood to the larger community.

The concept of telling our lives directly as a story offers us the power of the identity-building process. It is not only the powerful, those who control resources, who can write history. *The shift away from seeing oneself as powerless, as a victim of external circumstances, begins with telling one's own story.* Time after time, social change movements have begun the process of reshaping history and culture by creating stories. By articulating the hopes, dreams, and struggles of the disenfranchised, we ignite the spark of "what if" that can lead to direct action. When we feel a sense of outrage at individual and collective suffering, when we tell the stories of heroes, we can spark the desire to make a difference.

Those who work with minority and disadvantaged communities understand this but often do not know how to model change by speaking the truth in a way that is ongoing and meaningful. The use of storytelling circles and oral histories are fundamental and powerful tools for this task. For those techniques to be really effective, organizers and community members need to know how to listen to and tell difficult stories.

Lawyers

By the very nature of their work, lawyers are involved with difficult stories. This is true not only for trial lawyers but for those who practice family law. Often it is not the facts that are in dispute but the interpretation of those facts.

The conscious telling of the difficult story evokes image and emotional content. Lawyers often use a story as a "hook" to invite the listener into the tale by supplying motivation, offering an anticipation of what will come, and laying out the facts, as well as making connections between the listener and the litigants. Story invokes the power of prediction—how a particular resolution will heal, repair, or redress. It creates moments of decision, illuminating choices made and their impact on behaviors. It gives the facts of the case a human face.

The ability of lawyers to use this tool can be greatly enhanced by an understanding of the difficult story. The telling of the difficult story takes advantage of differing points of view and multiple interpretations of facts. It can focus the listener on single acts or particular moments. Story lingers; it brings language front and center. It lets the listener hear how something was said. It can recreate dialogue and tell how the words were meant. It invites the listener to consider "what if" and to identify the circumstance before him with his own experience.

—What We Are and What We Are Not— ——

Neither of us is a psychologist or a therapist. We are, instead, storytellers. It is impossible to be a storyteller without being a student of human nature. Loren has years of experience in community organizing and development. Elizabeth did long stint in public libraries—an excellent place to study human nature. Each of us has overcome struggles and experienced personal tragedies. Owning these events had made each of us a wiser and more compassionate person. Our work as storytellers reflects that.

The telling of difficult stories using the process presented in this book has been fulfilling for both of us. We believe there are ideas in this volume that will be helpful to many people. We do, however, recognize that this approach may not be appropriate for everyone. Some are too weary or too wounded for this process to be useful to them. Some will find that it raises more questions than it answers.

As you begin this work, we ask that you be kind to yourself. Do not ask of yourself that which you feel would be too demanding for someone else in your situation. Do not hesitate to seek help if ideas from this book bring up feelings that are too intense for you to deal with alone. This is particularly true as you tackle some of the exercises that are included in this book.

The telling of difficult stories is far from new. People told stories for thousands of years before the formal study of psychology evolved. In fact, those old stories are so powerful that Freud borrowed from them the terms used in therapy today. Even the term "psychology" itself comes from the story of Cupid and Psyche. In that story, the maiden Psyche wonders if her lover, Cupid, whom she has never seen, is human or a monster. Everyone who has ever been in a relationship has had that fear at some time. The question is, what to do when we are faced with it?

Like Freud and Jung, we will examine old traditional stories because they deal with primary human situations using metaphor with universal meaning. They also provide a blueprint for sharing stories effectively without the use of media or the printed page. They show us what works when you tell a story orally. Traditional folktales are models of compactness and directness. Paraphrasing that wonderful storyteller Augusta Baker, they begin simply, come to the point, and end swiftly and conclusively. There are no unnecessary words, but only the right ones to convey the beauty, the mood, the meaning of the tale.

We will also look at shaping stories from historical texts. Such material must often deal with the issues of racism and sexism. There is no way around the fact that as a species and as a nation, we have behaved badly in the past, or that people suffered and were denied opportunity because of their color or gender. It does no good to pretend it didn't happen. There is much to learn from an honest examination of this material that can then be transferred to all other types of stories.

We have included in this book a number of stories that the two of us tell. They include both adapted traditional and original material. In a few instances we have included stories from other tellers; when doing so we have acknowledged both the author and our reasons for including it. The stories are presented not only as examples but also as meditations on how we have responded to difficult topics. We own our words. We own the intent and meaning of our stories. They are chosen. They are crafted. They are told to particular audiences as both gift and lesson. We would hope that you would read them in a similar spirit.

Having said all that, if you are ready to begin we would recommend that you fasten your seatbelt. It may be a bumpy ride.

What is your reaction to hearing/reading a difficult story? What appeals to you? Where do you get stuck? Why do you embrace it or hold it at a distance?

Here is a list of the stories shared in this book:

- Loren Niemi's "By the Grace of God"
- Elizabeth Ellis's "Demeter and Persephone,1984'
- Loren Niemi's "Mitterand's Last Meal"
- Elizabeth Ellis's version of "Mister Fox"
- Loren Niemi's "Hansel and Gretel"
- Elizabeth Ellis's "Mary McLeod Bethune"
- Elizabeth Ellis's "Just Perfect"
- Loren Niemi's "Seeing Miss Julie"
- Megan Wells's "Thom's Dream"
- Loren Niemi's "Hannah on a Summer's Day"
- Tim Herwig's "Slaughter House"
- Loren Niemi's "The Rug"
- Elizabeth Ellis's "Political Prisoner"

Using this list, make some notes about your initial response to each story as you read it. What images or ideas are particularly appealing or challenging? What does it suggest or remind you of in your own life?

By their very nature, some difficult stories require some time to "hear" or understand. Give yourself a week or a month, then go back and reread these tales. Make a second set of notes about your responses after you've had time to "live" with them. Compare your first and second responses. What, if anything, has changed?

ONE

The Need to Shape and Artfully Tell the Difficult Story

That which would give light must endure burning.
—Victor Frankel

Why tell difficult stories? Isn't there enough violence and horror in the world without including it in our stories? Shouldn't we use storytelling to uplift and to celebrate what is right with the world?

We've been asked those questions and similar ones many times. While the specifics of our answer have changed over the years, the fundamental reasoning has not. We must tell difficult stories to be truly human. To be truly human is to acknowledge within our experience and imagination both sides of our nature. Spirit and flesh. Divine and profane. Hero and trickster.

The noted psychologist Carl Jung talked about the trickster as being both divine and profane. The trickster has his head in the clouds, his feet in the mud and everything in between is about pleasure and the problem of belly and sex. There is a little of Jung's trickster in each of us.

While we believe that it is both valuable and necessary to tell difficult stories, undertaking this work means making a journey that may not go directly to a safe harbor. As you read this book, or as you reflect with some care about the issues we raise, you may find yourself faced with personal emotional and psychological material that you were not prepared to consider. This is not necessarily a bad thing. Often issues come to our attention when we are able to face them. The opportunity to wrestle with the problem of how to tell the difficult story within a framework may be helpful to you.

In reading the stories we have included in this book, you may find that you do not like some of them. They do not speak to you or are, to use that word, difficult. Not every story will have the same relevance or meaning to every reader. Make a note of those that are troubling and put them aside. At some point you may want to examine what is troubling about them. What is the source of your discomfort—and more importantly, why? You may find that with some time and consideration, the meaning and appropriateness of these stories will shift.

It is too much to ask that you not be afraid. Instead, we ask that you proceed with caution. Be willing to take some risks, but keep in close touch with your feelings. If the feelings roused by the material in this book make you feel shaky, hang in there and continue to work on them. If, however, issues come up that overwhelm you, do not hesitate to get the support you need, whether it comes from friends or professionals. This is especially true if you choose to work the exercises.

What does thinking about or telling the truth of divorce, drug addiction, cancer, suicide, accident, or racism really mean to us? What lies beyond the sound bite of sensationalist media and the thin veneer of political correctness? How do we learn the impact and consequence of these kinds of events on people's real lives if we do not tell the difficult story?

If we do not tell our story, who will? Not as therapy or self-congratulation, but as direct testimony and transformation. Not out of guilt or titillation, but as part of the human experience from which we may draw lessons and model behaviors.

As a species, we have been very successful, and story has been fundamental to that dominion. We have used story to create external memory, to defeat death, and to pass the sum of our learning from one individual to the next, from one generation and culture to another. We have used story to shape the chaotic world through language and myth. We have acknowledged our connection with the world of spirit through that story we call religion, and to each other through the stories of identity and behavior we call history and law.

We have also been a very aggressive species—killing for survival, killing for sport, killing in the name of the stories of clan, race, religion, or political gestalt that give us our cultural identity. In many times and places, stories have justified and celebrated the spilling of blood.

From *Gilgamesh* to *Beowulf,* stories tell us what heroes do. From the call to the Crusades to the contemporary media coverage of the latest exercise in geopolitical intervention, the call to patriotism harnesses story to its ends. On the one hand there are the stories that make the enemy the "other," a brutal and inhuman threat to our cherished way of life, who must be defeated by any means necessary. In WWII America, the racist stories of the "yellow peril" made it easier to accept, without question, the placement of native-born citizens of Japanese descent in concentration camps.

On the other, there are the stories of bravery and sacrifice we tell to inspire our youth to fight the good fight for country, flag, and our way of life. No matter that the enemy is telling the same kind of stories in hopes that they will prevail. It is often said that you cannot see the enemy as a faceless other, as a monster when you know their story. It does not mean that we agree with them or approve of their beliefs or actions. In knowing their story, we can understand how they arrived at their views and why they act as they do. In the best of circumstances, we can also see how they are just like us—human, fallible, trying to do their best for family and homeland.

If history and politics are difficult to consider, why not turn to the comfort of the traditional tales of entertainment? There is no reprieve here. What is "Hansel and Gretel"? A pleasant folktale to be told to children? A candy house with a cardboard-cutout witch in the window? Or is it the story of abused children left by parents who no longer can bear the burden of raising them? A bitter lesson on the necessity of self-reliance? Is it the historical document of well-founded fears, held at a slight distance, to help children understand the real toll of poverty and dysfunctional family life? Take a good look at the text from the Brothers Grimm and you'll see the disturbing story that stands at the core—a story of hunger, hard lessons, even murder leading to "happily ever after." It never was a story free of shadow or terror, and why should it be?

In many ways, the essence of the difficult story is shadow and terror. In looking at what we fear we may come to understand its power and its falsity. In traditional cultures it was understood that to name something was to have power over it. In the Book of Genesis, when God places Adam in the garden, the confirmation of Adam's dominion over the natural world is God's command that he should name it.

Tabloid culture has taught us to look for the kind of story that dwells on the difficult. It follows the old news dictum that "what bleeds, leads." It presents scandal as ubiquitous and commonplace. It gives us violence and gore but does not help us understand why these things happen or what tragedy or evil might mean to those involved. What do the details of folly mean to those who hear the tales? There seems to be a growing taste for sensationalism, scandal, and confession in our culture while the complex reality of human experience remains unexamined.

Within this book's scope, we want you to arrive at a place where you can honestly speak the truth about your experience of any difficult story. We are not asking that you embrace the sensational or the scandalous. We are not asking you to make a public confession. If anything, we are asking that you choose topics and stories that speak to the best and truest sense of what it means to be human. It may not always be clear why a given story is important and deserves to be told. It will not always be clear when this story is ready to be told. Even with the use of the exercises, that process will unfold as quickly or as slowly as is necessary for you to come to understand the shape and meaning of your own stories.

As we said before, to do this may require courage on your part and the willingness to examine your responses thoughtfully and compassionately. It may be frustrating. You may get scared or angry. Sometimes journaling, drawing, pillow-punching, or a good cry will be enough. At other times you may wish to reach out to someone you can talk to about any of the issues or feelings that may come to the surface as you are going through this process. If necessary, we would recommend that you discuss your experience, your feelings, with a professional, whether it is a counselor, minister, or therapist. Remember, there is a fine line between challenging yourself to grow and damaging yourself by overextension or carelessness.

It seems to us that in choosing to tell difficult stories, whether they be personal stories or traditional folktales, the difficult material needs to be dealt with as having substance and weight.

That is because it does. If we are to tell traditional material such as "Little Red Riding Hood" or "Cinderella," we need to find the beating heart and emotional center of these stories that have too often become a sugar candy of plot without content. These stories did not survive by being weak or powerless to engage imagination and emotion at the deepest levels. Where does the desire to devour or the need to be recognized meet the fear of discovery or loss?

If we strip stories, whether personal or traditional, of their meaning because we are afraid, we not only do a disservice to the stories, but ultimately to the listener and to ourselves. To assume that listeners cannot understand the meaning of a story or will not be prepared to deal with difficult material is to deny the richness and complexity of people's real lives.

As much as we need to tell the difficult story, there are those who need to hear it. For many, the very fact that these topics might be spoken of serves as a beacon of hope or reassurance that they are not alone. In a world where families suffer prejudice, economic hardship, illness, accident, and untimely death, listeners need ways to understand and acknowledge their suffering as part of the human experience, not be denied its power or the necessity of their coming to grips with it.

Here is a story to illustrate what we mean by "difficult." It is the story of discovery of one's place in the universe.

LOREN NIEMI ——

By the Grace of God

In the late '60s, when I was driving taxi, eager to make the next dollar, and before urban renewal leveled the flophouses to make way for parking lots, I was living on Nicollet Island. It was a piece of rundown history in Minneapolis with more than its share of derelict buildings. Yet at its center, there was a temple of the spirit amid the city's hustle and bustle. Not a church, mind you. No, I had learned long ago that true temples are not made of brick and stone. It was more a manifest space than a formal place denoted by orthodoxy and decor.

Hidden beside the edge of the Mississippi River, :hind the warehouses and within sight of the hobo jungle, w : a little garden of delight that was the very embodiment of iana's sacred grove, the bower of Merlin, the last reposi ry of Nature's wild spirit. Amid the sound of industry, the rrible gnashing of progress, was a place where fairies migh lance and Puck would be proud to roam. Holy ground. Sa1 tuary where the fulsome clang and clamor of the city was sul 1med to the song of the bullfrog surveying lazy water in h)es of finding a bluebottle fly. Sylvan light danced upon t : lazy waters, and the stillness of air contained the myriad s1 lls of earth, air, fire, and water. Spiders worked their craft tu weave gossamer spirit-catchers while acolyte hummingbirds attended to the altar bouquets. I had passed the place a hundred times and not seen it for what it was, but like all holy places, it was seen to best advantage when it was seen with a guide.

My guide was Tommy the Wino.

Before I shifted to driving nights, every day began the same way. I'd come down the long dark stair from my little flat and out to the hustle of the street. Go ten feet, maybe twenty feet, and Tommy would appear. He'd step out of the shadow of a doorway and stick out his hand. The cracked-skin palm, the missing finger. I always knew it was Tommy. Everyone on the island knew him. Never said anything. No come-on, no sad story about how he needed bus fare to a job interview or was collecting spare change to buy a parting gift for a dying mother. Just the hand, empty, waiting to be filled, and the thousand-yard stare of a man who knew that guilt worked best when it was left to find its own resting place.

Sometimes I'd give him a dime or a quarter. Sometimes not. Made no difference to him. If you gave, he didn't acknowledge it, he simply removed the coin from sight. If you didn't give, the hand simply floated in your wake, a reminder of a lost opportunity for the milk of human kindness. Day in, day out, rain or shine, he was there. It didn't matter if I went another way or crossed the street, sooner or later the hand appeared with expectation in attendance.

One day I decide to cut to the chase. Forget the unspoken asking, forget the waiting for enough. The hand appeared, and as soon as it did, I clasped it.

Hey, man, this is your lucky day, I said, as I reeled Tommy out of the shadows.

What? A croak like a frog with a bellyache. Tommy blinked in the sunlight and shrugged off the arm I put around his shoulder. Don't touch, OK? I don't like to be touched.

OK. So, here's the deal Tommy, I'm goin' up the block into Mitch's and I'm going to buy a bottle. You can pick the bottle and I'll pay.

No shit?

No shit, I said as we turned in the door of Mitch's Liquor. The place was a monument to mistrust. The place was nothing more than a long box with a set of shelves on each wall and a cash register at the far end. Running the length of the store was a chain link fence separating the customers from the merchandise. If you wanted something, you called to Mitch or his ugly brother, George, and pointed through the hard wire at your choice. They would pick it off the shelf, go back to the cashier's cage, tell you the price. You dropped your money into the little trough. They would scoop up the bills, or more often, the coins, count them out and put the brown bagged bottle of choice in a little box contraption that opened on your side to let you remove your fondest desire. The entire transaction was a ritual of psychic abuse that the brothers relished and the winos put up with. Why? The sad fact was that if you could point and put the coin on the counter, you got a bottle no matter your age or condition.

Tommy was pressed against the fence, his eyes gazing with the fondness of a loving father for his children as he beheld the promise in those rows of green glass jugs and fortified wines.

Anything you want, Tommy. Just pick your poison and I'm good for the price.

Irish Rose, he said, pointing at a squat green bottle on the bottom shelf.

Really? Not something from the next shelf up?

I like it.

Hey, you down there, this man wants a bottle of your finest Irish Rose.

Three sixty-eight. That was the price of Tommy's habit. Fifteen quarters would do the trick. If you could cat four bucks an hour, you could work one, take a couple of o celebrate, and repeat as needed. Three sixty-eight, arrive t that number maybe two, three times a day and there yo were. Immune to pain. Drinking to forget until you were gone you forgot to drink. I certainly would have chosen something a little higher up the price spread, but I wanted a taste of his world, not mine.

Back out on the street, Tommy headed for the Avenue

Bridge. He slipped down the little embankment to a wide spot where the rough stone arch supports rose from the ground. We walked to the far side of the bridge footings, out of the sun. Tommy settled down with his back to the stone support, looking at a little scrub of paper birch trees providing the opportunity for the soft flutter of leaves in the breeze. I settled in next to him and took a look at his chosen haven.

There was a thicket of cattails at the water's edge and a spray of wildflowers, mostly columbines and bee balm, that began where the cattails ended. Butterflies danced the processional across flickering motes of sunlight while the frogs croaked a welcome along the water's edge. Behind and above us was the manmade world of bridge steel, where pigeons nested in the girders, raising their young to the steady rumble and vibration of commerce. Before us was the last vestige of the real river. The nominally slow current squeezed into a twisted swirl of swift-moving water, washing boulders and highway abutments, except for one little eddy pool where I could see the shimmer of fish—maybe catfish, but more likely carp or bullheads—just below the warm suede surface. Along the side of the green velvet pools, with dragonflies glittering like small jewels, stood pale crowds of cattails and the plentiful tracks of raccoons who dined at riverside by night.

I handed Tommy the bag. He slipped the top down just enough to reveal the tax stamp, cracked the seal and threw the cap into the water. Not one to stand on ceremony or conversation, he hoisted the bottle and took a good swallow.

He handed the bag back to me. For a moment, I hesitated to wipe the rim, but caught him nodding approval from the corner of my eye. As I brought the bottle to my lips I noticed a piece of lint had caught on the edge. I tilted the bottle back and felt the lint on the tip of my tongue. I tasted the blue cotton work shirt and in the instant that followed the harsh burning of the fortified wine swept the cotton into my throat, where it held on for dear life. I simultaneously coughed a good portion of the wine into my nose and swallowed the lint.

Good stuff, Tommy said, taking the bottle from my hand.

We sat there for a good long time, not saying much. The sun was warm, the soft lapping of the water on the shore mixed with the deeper vibration of the heavy trucks and buses crossing the bridge. For a brief moment, in a lifetime of odd moments dimly appreciated in the present but cherished in retrospect, we passed the gut-wrenching fire back and forth. There was a sense of the world as complete, satisfying and in its place. I drank a little less with each pass of the bag, while Tommy's satisfied smile grew larger with each sip. The ephemeral and transitory world slipping away, he entered into the twilight of Bacchus, a trance state as close to bliss as his worn body would allow. Finally, he held the bottle upside down and shook out the last drops.

For the river spirits, he said.

We got to our feet, or tried to. I felt the rush of bad wine like a shudder when the freight train starts as the weight of loaded boxcars resists the notion of movement. The blood drained from my head, and earth called me home. Suddenly I understood the meaning of the word *swoon*, as my legs gave way under me and I went down, powerless to exert my will and clutching for something firm to hold on to.

Tommy reached over, grabbed my arm with a g   ) that was surprisingly firm for a man who looked like he v   s half past dead. Yah, I used to do that when I stood up. T   igh it out, you'll get used to falling.

No sooner had he said it when he looked at his own hand on my arm and snatched it away. He smiled an embarrassed smile, ran his hands through his stubble field of gray hair, turned and walked away without goodbye or thank you.

For the next few days, I didn't see him on the street. No hand floating from the shadows. No Tommy. I began to wonder if I had offended him in some way, perhaps I hadn't shown the proper respect for the ritual of sharing a bottle or failed to observe some wino protocol. When I finally caught a glimpse of him half a block away I had to run to catch up.

Hey, Tommy, how come I don't see you any more? You haven't asked me for dime one in a week now. What gives?

He stopped and took a long look at me. Then he shook his head like I was the village idiot asking for an explanation of why the sun rises and sets. You bought the bottle, man. You shared joy juice with Tommy. I couldn't ask you for money—you're one of us.

Many audiences have a difficult time with "By the Grace of God." It discomforts them even as it makes them laugh. Many of us have no desire to move the homeless out of the box we have put them in. We need them to remain "other," in order to remind ourselves of how lucky we are. They serve as an object lesson we can offer children of what happens when you don't study or work hard. They remind us of the wages of sin or moral weakness. The last thing we want to see them as is ourselves in another circumstance.

The hardest part of hearing "By the Grace of God" is the ending. Really understanding that we as well as they may be "one of us." The difference between Tommy and any member of the audience may be nothing more than circumstance and bad choices. But it is precisely this realization—that less separates us from the homeless or the alcoholic than we generally assume—that can make the story meaningful.

Storytellers, especially platform tellers, often complain that festival and theatrical performance audiences are "so small, so uniformly white, and so middle class." Where is the rest of the community, they ask? We respond, could part of the problem be that they tell (predominately) humorous and nostalgic tales that non-white and non-middle class audiences don't recognize as speaking to and for their lives?

In working with communities of color, Loren has been told that they do not want a passing nod to their cultural traditions. What they hunger for is a living, breathing understanding of the everyday lives they live and the struggles they face in the present.

It is by directly dealing with the difficult story that we invite the audience to share common ground in the present. It is this creating of common ground that builds community and resolves problems. It is in the honest examination of difficult topics that we name oppression for what it is and heal our wounds. It is in shared understanding that the therapeutic story moves from being the story of the self to the story of the community and the species.

We should clarify here the difference between therapy and therapeutic stories. The joke is that in therapy we pay the audience and in storytelling the audience pays us. We all have difficulties. One of the crucial functions of therapy is to give us a chance to tell, understand, and in many cases edit our story to change our feelings and behavior. This process is best done with the help of people you trust. It is best done in private.

It is not appropriate for storytellers of any stripe to do personal therapy with an unsuspecting listener. Whether you are in the classroom, at the office, or on a public stage, the difficult story you want to share should be already worked out. What story-tellers tell their listeners is a therapeutic story whose meaning is clear and accessible to the listener.

If it is not, then the least you can do is ask the listener if they are willing to act as a sounding board for work in progress. What you tell in the workplace should not presume participation of your fellow workers in group therapy. What you work on as therapy to arrive at that universal, therapeutic story, is done in private—with friends, professionals, or small groups who give you permission to flail about in search of the right words and the right image. These people understand they are there to help you test and let you fail, then reshape the story until you get it right.

Coming to understand the meaning of your experience and shaping it to be shared is an appropriate and permissible thing to do. But we should be clear that the choice of what to tell, how and when to tell it, should be done in a controlled environment.

The therapeutic story is not about making the listener squirm, want to run away, or pity you. It is not about your losing control or trying to use your listeners as an involuntary sounding board while you try to understand what happened and what it means. It is about making a gift of story to them. It is about the opportunity for the listener to identify with the emotional core and meaning of our common human experience in the particular story being told.

—The Value of Speaking Truthfully—

There is a value in speaking truthfully. It is, too often, a rare and precious commodity. It is so much easier to fudge, to hedge our bets, to gloss off the rough edges. But to what purpose? Does it make difficulty any easier to understand or resolve?

When we decide to tell the difficult story, we are facing that which would be denied. We know from the testimony of both victims and perpetrators that silence makes abuse possible. It is handmaiden to shame and allows those who would abuse permission to continue. It holds those that are abused in harm's way. We know from the testimony of both those who are addicted and those who turn their heads, trying to hold the effect of addiction at a distance, that denial postpones recovery.

Our observation would be that silence about the difficult situations in our lives poisons the well. It taints our ability to see clearly and denies us balance. It makes us vulnerable to illness and accident. So the decision to tell the difficult story, and to tell it truthfully, is a decision for clarity, health, and balance.

This is not always easy. It takes courage to see that there is a story to be told. It takes additional courage to decide to tell it. Once you decide to do so, it takes some care to shape the story in such a way as it can be heard for what it is. Sometimes you have to admit to your own faults, your foolishness or vulnerability. Sometimes you have to acknowledge failure or guilt. There is always the possibility of shame and embarrassment. But as the Bible verse says, the truth shall set you free.

—Personal Meaning and Shared Meaning—

Metaphor moves us from one realm to another. It takes us from a personal meaning to a shared one. Being fully cognizant and fully engaged in the process of telling our lives and the world as we truthfully know it can be done through a literal narrative or a figurative one. Which should we use? Choose the one that best serves the needs of the story.

We can do this directly as personal narrative or as oral history. We can do this indirectly as allegory or metaphor. In either case, by facing the difficult situation and being able to tell the truth about it, we move first to understanding and then to resolution. To fully tell the truth we must say that we have experienced so-and-so, that we felt such-and-such. Hopefully we do so in ways that let those we are speaking to identify it as part of their experience as well.

Some of us (often in name of Truth) want to avoid the shadow side of our experience and think that by focusing only on the positive, we can set a good example. Admitting that we are capable of great folly and evil, as well as the good and the heroic, is a healthy and often a humorous experience. Human beings are not immune to change, contradiction, or mistake. In recognizing this within ourselves, we come to understand that these are also keys to our survival and growth as a species. Through story, we can learn from our experience.

In acknowledging the shadow side, we do not necessarily need to make a confession; we can choose to explore the darkness within us by means of metaphor, allegory, and parable. We can employ a host of literary techniques developed over the centuries to make it easier to hear and recognize our folly.

When we speak of metaphor, one of its functions is to name that which cannot be dealt with directly.

This is especially true within traditional stories. Many generations shared both the light and shadow of life whether they were in the peasant's farmhouse or the landlord's manor. There were few secrets, but even they must be spoken for the sake of justice. The use of metaphor is a sleight of hand that informs the folktales. The wandering balladeers and storytellers found ways of speaking the hard truth of daily life without wearing out their welcome. Or the slave might transpose that traditional African trickster, Hare, into Br'er Rabbit, and Massa' would enjoy it so much he'd want to have it told to his children. Did he recognize Br'er Fox? Did he hear the recipe for hope and resist-ance in the tales of the sly rabbit who outwitted his tormentors?

The great value of metaphor is that is takes the personal and opens it to a larger sense of connection with the world. Human beings are driven by sense. We measure the world in terms of how it looks, sounds, smells, tastes, and feels. When we say that we were "chilling" or we were "spitting into the wind" we do not mean that we were actually getting cold or testing our understanding of aerodynamics. These are metaphors that expand our access to information by substituting one image for another. The appeal to the senses provides a concept to which we can apply meaning.

When metaphor can make a connection between our expe-rience or internal feelings and the world of the senses, it serves as a bridge for understanding. It provides us with images that help us grasp the significance, the meaning of something. It allows those who are ready to hear, to hear. It allows us t move from personal to shared meaning.

Here is a story to illustrate what we mean by "moving from personal to shared meaning" and, in the process, making con-nection between a classical myth and the everyday world in which we live.

ELIZABETH ELLIS

Demeter and Persephone, 1984

I traveled to Missouri to tell stories at a festival, leaving my fifteen-year-old daughter Robin at home with her big brother, Scooter. When I returned, she was gone. I asked Scooter when he had last seen her. He said he had not seen her since I left. I was furious. I asked, "Why didn't you call and tell me that?"

He said, "If I had done that, you would have rushed

home in the middle of the festival. You would have upset a lot of people and probably damaged your career. When you got here, there wouldn't have been anything for you to do that I haven't already done. I reported her missing to the police. I've been to see each of her friends. If they aren't talking to me, they sure aren't talking to you."

It would be weeks before I would be willing to admit that he was right.

I thought she must have run away from home with the boy she had been dating, but there was no way I could be sure. Perhaps she was lying face down in a ditch somewhere. I could not get the image out of my mind. I made the rounds of all her friends. It was as fruitless and frustrating as Scooter had said it would be.

I drove over to the apartment complex where Robin's boyfriend had been living with his family. I sat in my car for a long time getting up the courage to knock on their door. I put my head down on the steering wheel of my car and prayed. Finally, I went up and knocked on the door. The force of my knock sent the unlatched door swinging open. I stepped inside. Before me was complete emptiness, bare carpet staring back at me. I ran back to my car and put my head down on the steering wheel again. This time I did not pray, I wept.

The days kept dragging by. I could not sleep. I could not work. I jumped up each time the phone rang, certain it would be her. It never was.

One day the police called. They said they had found a body of a young girl. It was about my daughter's size and age and coloring. They wanted me to come to the morgue to look at the body.

I threw some clothes on and drove myself downtown. I

walked down a set of marble steps to the basement and down a long empty corridor. I signed my name on a clipboard. They led me into the coldest room I have ever entered. There were stainless steel doors in each wall. I remember the detective was a kind man. Just before he pulled out the drawer, he reached down and took my hand.

It was not my daughter. But it was someone's daughter. I could not bear the idea that they would be burying her in a pauper's grave. I got on the phone and began calling my friends. I asked them to help me give her a proper funeral with a minister and flowers and music. While I was making the calls, the police found the girl's parents in a suburb of Houston. I have never met them, but I still pray for them.

Several weeks later, a lady asked me to do some work for an event she was chairing. She said planning this charity function was really keeping her busy. If I would meet her for lunch, she could get more work done and have a real to boot. So I drove over to one of Dallas's wealthiest neighborhoods to eat lunch at a place where I would not ordinarily go.

Just as we sat down in a front booth, a young woman charged past us carrying a big round tray. She said, "I'll be right back to get your order—Mom."

And there was my daughter. One look at her expanded silhouette, and I knew she was going to have a baby. I have thought about it for years, but I have never figured out anything I ever said or did that would make her think she couldn't share that information with me from the beginning. She said she was afraid I would be angry. I told her I was grateful to know that she was alive.

When fall came, I gave a public concert. I was pleased with the attendance, about fifty people. During intermission a woman told me she had attended my spring concert and enjoyed it very much. She said her sister was visiting from Detroit. She wondered if I would tell "Demeter and Persephone." She said she had been so moved by it in the spring, she would like her sister to hear it.

I had learned the story in the spring because I thought it would be a useful story to know. By now I had told it many times, both to children and adults. I was confident I could remember it, even though I had not told it in some time, so I agreed to her request.

By the time the audience returned to their seats, I had decided to begin with that story. I started to tell how Demeter returned home and found Persephone missing. She searched everywhere for her, but could not find her. I remembered how the ancient text said she went looking for her daughter, and her grief was so great that wherever she walked the grass died beneath her feet. I knew exactly how that felt. I knew what it was like to go to the land of the dead looking for your child. I had been there. I still remembered what it smelled like. I knew there was no three-headed dog at the entrance. There was a guy eating a fish sandwich who wanted your signature on a clipboard. I knew exactly what Persephone was going to look like when Demeter found her with a tag on her toe.

The story kept picking up speed and it kept picking up power. It was coming out of my gut like a runaway freight train headed straight for my listeners. That part of me that is the observer could look out at them, sitting at a forty-five degree angle with every hair on their heads blown straight back from the force of the story. I could feel sorry for them, but I could not stop. I am convinced if I had stopped telling at that moment, I would have dropped dead of a heart attack. So I told it. I told it to the bloody end.

When I finished, the whole group made a little gasping noise. Then there was dead silence in the room for a moment. Nearly everyone wiped their eyes. Then they started standing up and putting on their jackets. Even though it was the first story I had told after the intermission, they began collecting their things. They stood around me in a tight little circle. They did not speak to me, but they spoke about me. "That's her sweater. I saw her wearing it when she arrived." "This must be her purse."

They formed a tight knot around me and walked me out to the parking lot. A man stepped forward and said, "I don't think she should drive." Another man said, "She can ride with my wife, and I will drive her car home for her."

When we reached my house, they unlocked the door for me and asked if they should call someone to come and be with me. I told them I was feeling better and would be all right.

You probably think all those people would be afraid to come back to hear me tell stories. You would be wrong. If I advertise that I will be telling stories for adults, I can count on seeing many of them. They are kind to me, and tight with one another, like people are who have been to boot camp together. Over the years, we've even had a couple of weddings within that group. But none of them ever asks me to tell "Demeter and Persephone."

I haven't told the story since. I am still working on it. When I am ready to tell it, I can promise you people will remember that they heard it.

—The Value of Speaking Artfully———

In telling a difficult story, the choice to tell it is not sufficient unto itself. The source material must be shaped. What matters is the careful and conscious process of making a "story" out of the raw material of our lives. Therapy is coming to understand what happened in your personal history. Therapy is coming to understand why. Therapy is coming to reframe your beliefs, values, behaviors for yourself. But therapy is not making art.

Story is art. Story is about not being limited by the facts in order to tell the truth. Story is about crafting the facts, what is said and what is not said, to make the meaning of an experience clear. Story as art is about integrating the world of what happens with the world of why it does so. For art to be therapeutic, it first and foremost must be the conscious creation of order out of *chaos* for the sake of meaning. It is arranging images to appeal to the senses as a way of seeing what is beneath the surface or what might be.

To choose to tell the difficult story as therapy requires no art, but often, as we said before, some degree of courage. To tell the difficult story as art in a public venue—whether in performance, in the courtroom, or in the classroom—is a choice to tell a conscious construction for the benefit of the listener. It should not be seen as a choice to tell your personal history unless that history has been understood and shaped to move beyond a personal meaning.

Often the very process of choosing to shape and tell the story is enough to free us from the constraints that we impose upon ourselves and provides ways for us to see how we have limited our understanding. It requires us to ask, what is the meaning of this experience? Does it make sense? How do I convey to others the sense of time and place, of emotion and action that made it important to me? How do I appeal to the senses? Which facts and details can best convey the story I want to share?

If shaping is inevitable, and it is, we should strive to have it be well crafted. The very act of telling of those portions of our experience where we have been tried and survived or failed is valuable. Where we embrace the shadow, the testimony of what happened next can be life-affirming. To speak the truth and to speak the art, we may need to put into the story sensory appeals, metaphors, references, or themes that help the listener make a connection to the meaning. We may need to move beyond the facts. To speak truth and art, we may need to leave out of the story those things that confuse the listener or may be so private as to be meaningless to anyone but yourself.

Here is a story to illustrate what we mean by "artful shaping of material." It begins with a literary reference and has a story within the story to give a metaphoric shape to the whole.

————————————————————————————— LOREN NIEMI —

Mitterand's Last Meal

Oh, Wolf, she said, let me bite you.

Bite me? Really? Sniff for sniff? Nuzzle for nuzzle? Lick for lick? Bite for bite? Down to the flesh? Down to the bone?

Yes, she said, I am very hungry.

I was driving from Minneapolis to Chicago on one of those snowy days when the flakes come down large, white, singular, each falling with a soft plop against the windshield. It was not a heavy snow, but it was a messy one, and the car was already skidding across the surface of the road at fifty-five to sixty miles an hour. In the rearview mirror I could see an eighteen-wheeler coming up behind me, fast, seventy to eighty miles an hour, its lights wildly careering through the white. As it passed, it sprayed the windshield with a heavy black slush. In that moment, as the windshield wipers struggled to clear a view and the car slid sideways, I was catapulted to another time, to another moment some months before when I had stopped in Milwaukee to see my lover and tell her that it was over.

We were having lunch in a German restaurant when she began weeping into her borscht. I had not spoken those words of ending yet but her tears fell in such profusion that it took me a while to understand that she was lamenting the death of her favorite aunt. The woman who had inspired her was gone and there was no consolation. I held her hand and bit my tongue. Later I drove aimlessly around the block until she was done crying and could return to her office, never once having said the words of finality I had intended to speak.

Driving away, I turned on the radio. It was "This American Life" with Ira Glass. It was the annual "poultry" show—stories about chickens and other fowl. Not much caught my attention until they came to the story of Mitterand's last meal. François Mitterand, the President of France, dying of cancer, called together thirty-two of his closest friends for a sumptuous last dinner. He did not include his wife—or his mistress. His guests sat at one table eating the oysters, the good breads, the rich pâté de foi gras, drinking the fine wines and pastel-colored sorbets between courses, all working toward the final course.

The President sat at a table by himself. He would eat a little, drink a little, then pass out. They would let him sleep until the next course was served. Finally, the last course came, the serving of ortolan, a small French songbird. It is illegal to eat this delicacy, a traditional meal of kings that has been banned since the Revolution. By custom, the bird is eaten with a napkin over one's head so that "God and France may not see your shame."

The bird itself is small, about the size of your thumb. It is captured live, force fed, and then drowned in liquor before it is plucked and baked whole. It is customary to eat the bird in its entirety—head, organs, bones, and all.

The writer whom Ira Glass was interviewing had described Mitterand's last meal for an *Esquire* magazine article and later tried it to duplicate it. He had to call a hundred chefs before he found one who would agree to cook it. Even that chef placed a stipulation on the meal that they could not eat the head; they had to put it back on the plate because he still had some scruples.

Ira asked what was it like, and the writer said, "It was white. Wearing the white napkin, my field of vision was limited," he said, "to the plate, which was also white, and on the plate the small brown speck of the bird. The napkin concentrated the intense aroma of the roasted flesh of the ortolan. I picked the bird up, bit off the head, which I spit back onto the plate, and began to chew.

"The first taste was of meat so sweet and delicate I had never experienced anything like it before. Suddenly there was the burst of hot liqueur from inside the bird, scalding the back of my throat, and then it got harder. There was the bitter taste of the organs but I continued to chew. Finally I was chewing on the bones and I had to decide whether or not I should swallow or spit them out, but I had come this far and did not want to be shamed, so I swallowed."

The writer went on to say that if every meal had to be eaten with as much consciousness as that one was, we would starve to death. It certainly was the case for Mitterand, who ate the ortolan and then let no other food pass his lips. He died three days later. At his funeral, his wife stood on one side of his casket and his mistress and his daughter by her on the other.

It was raining as I listened to this. I rolled the window down and the late November smell of Lake Michigan filled the car. At the instant a potent mix—dead fish, seaweed, wet concrete, diesel, the decay of autumn—filled the car. I thought about what it would be like to eat the bird, sensing the shape and weight of the warm body in my mouth, my teeth working through tender flesh. Thought about what it is to swallow the forbidden, to taste the bitter organs and bone. To be conscious of the devouring.

A semi comes by on the right and sprayed the windshield with gray water obscuring my vision. The windshield wipers struggled to keep up. The car shuddered.

Oh, Wolf, she said, let me bite you.

Really? Sniff for sniff? Nuzzle for nuzzle? Lick for lick? Bite for bite? Down to flesh? Down to bone?

Yes, she said, I am very hungry.

The smell of the lake, the smell of cold water, the smell of the warm flesh, the smell of her perfume, filled the car. I tasted my own desire and in that moment all I could do was think to myself, how good it was to be alive.

In the presentation of the difficult topic there are times when the best approach is to create the troubled landscape and then point out its features by analogy. Is ending an illicit relationship really like eating a bitter morsel? Do we really jump back and forth in time from one moment to another? Not really, but they convey through vivid sense imagery the context for understanding the story.

Suggested Further Reading

Frankel, Victor. *Man's Search for Meaning*. Boston: Beacon Press, 1992.

Simpkinson, Charles and Anne. *Sacred Story: A Celebration of the Power of Stories to Transform and Heal*. San Francisco: HarperSanFrancisco, 1993.

Down one side of a page make a list of the difficult story topics at right. Next to them identify if you are now telling stories about that topic or whether you would want to tell a story around that topic.

What are your own personal reasons for not telling difficult stories? Taking some time to journal about them can be a valuable experience. It can:

• provide clarity and greater focus;

• give voice to what has remained unnamed and unexamined;

• be motivational, offering a sense of vision or mission;

• help prioritize issues.

Do not skimp on the time necessary to write fully about your reasons. Taking the time to do this thoroughly at the beginning may prove to be a valuable resource in the future.

violence
rape
murder
betrayal
revenge
abuse
divorce
alcoholism
drug addiction
masturbation
incest
adultery
homosexuality
despair
suicide
pride
gluttony
sloth
theft
anger
lust
envy
racism
prejudice
illness
death
natural disaster
accident
disability

TWO

Self-Censorship

There's an ocean of words that got caught in my throat.
I'm gonna let loose the waters and learn how to float.
—Betsy Rose

There are stories in which we find a home. They are welcoming and comfortable. We feel secure in them. They are cozy in our hearts and on our tongues. There are others that plague us like some uninvited guest. They whisper to us in voices so persistent that it is a struggle to ignore them. Others take us emotional hostage and will not let us go until we accede to their demands. There are also tales that enter our consciousness like a SWAT team, suddenly and by surprise. However they arrive, we need to understand that they will affect us and our view of the world.

The comfortable stories are easy to tell; they slip out of our mouths readily. Others, though we long to tell them, will not pass our lips without a struggle. Some seem stuck crossways in our throats. If we try to tell them, they come out in some muddled mass that makes sense to no one, including ourselves.

What is it that catches in our throats and stills our tongues? There are many issues that bring us to an uneasy silence

Emotions: We feel embarrassed by what we have done or failed to do. The story arouses such strong feelings in us that we are afraid we will lose control in front of others. Our shame makes us secretive. We are not ready to face ourselves, or at least how we have behaved in a given situation.

Confusion: We are still too closely involved. We have not processed the experience. We have no point of entry into the story. We do not know how to exit it, or if it even has an end. We do not know how to shape it. We do not understand what it means.

Other People: We do not believe anyone else would be interested in our story. We believe our stories are too painful to tell and therefore will be too painful for others to hear. We do not want to offend. We wish to protect our family or our friends. We are concerned about being criticized. We are afraid of being misunderstood. We are terrified others really *will* understand.

Punishment: We are afraid of being censured. We are concerned about being fired. We fear being excommunicated. We are concerned we will not be asked back. We might severely limit our marketability. We are sure we will end up as homeless vagrants or bag ladies.

Whether the reasons we give for not telling difficult stories appear to be internal or external, we should examine them. No cursory glance will tell us what we need to know. It is important to be completely honest with ourselves about the reasons we hesitate and the necessity to not do so. Without honesty, the truest and deepest reasons that silence us will remain unexamined.

No matter what form our reasons may take, they are based on fear. Fear is the great shape-shifter. Though it can change itself into many forms, its essence always remains the same: it is about hesitation. Careful inspection usually helps us see this.

A rigorous examination of our reasons has much to teach us about ourselves. We may find that we are more in need of the approval of others than we realized. We could make discoveries about our relationships that would be valuable to know.

If you are holding back because you are trying to avoid criticism, rest assured that someone will criticize you no matter what you do. If you are concerned about offending, remember that half the people will be offended because you said too much, and the other half will be equally offended because you said too little. All truth tellers and prophets are unwelcome. Criticism and misunderstanding are unavoidable, especially if you are committed to a public expression of human experience.

Confusion and lack of clarity can be worked through. Creative steps can be taken to protect friends and family.

Economic considerations may not be as strong as we imagined. There is an audience for every story, but we may have to leave safety behind in order to find it. There are people who would gladly pay to hear the story of their lives affirmed. The basis of AA and Twelve Step groups is to provide the opportunity for anyone to speak the hard truth they have lived to those who could tell it as well. The impulse to tell safe stories may not make us financially poorer, but it impoverishes the spirit and denies the crucial historical role of stories in teaching us the ways of the world.

Often the most negative reaction we receive comes from some of our peers. It would be wonderful to receive only support from our colleagues. Unfortunately, those entrenched in the status quo do not take well to change. We are always going to be engaged in educating our peers. We are always going to have to explain, defend, or ignore the criticism of what we are doing by those who are afraid to risk. Which would you prefer: a peer who says "Nobody would ever want to hear that!" or to hear the voice of the story that keeps calling out to be told by you? Think about your priorities.

Storytelling is an art form. Perhaps because it is so fundamental to human experience we forget what that means. If everyone tells stories, you say, where is the art in it?

Think seriously about storytelling as art. It is the most basic and accessible of all our art forms. It is an act of pure creation. It is experience and imagination made manifest in language. It uses both sides of our brain. It invites one member of the species to appreciate and understand another. It has the power to elicit physical and emotional connections and response.

If storytelling is an art form, and you are telling stories, what does that say about you? You are an artist. Own that for a moment. If you are a storyteller, you are an artist.

It is important to think of ourselves as artists. When we begin to do that, a lot of choices begin to fall into place quite naturally. The work of an artist is not always popular but it must be done. It's not always easy; it's not always accepted. Marshall McLuhan said that artists are "the antennae of the race," providing the early warning signals of cultural change. If you are an artist, your work is important. It is a service to the community. Making art is a necessity for our physical and spiritual health. That which calls out to be told by you deserves to be told. It deserves to be honored. It deserves to be respected. By you first of all.

Which of your experiences are unique? What do you have to say that can only be said by you? The universal is contained in the specific. No one else sees the world in quite the same way you do. You have your own unique work, and it calls out to be done. We live in a sad and sorry world. We are a grieving nation, and we have much to grieve for. You have something to say. There is an unbroken continuum between the personal immediate, the everyday, and the timeless primal, the mythic. Our world is hungry for that which would nurture us and give us hope.

Art is about taking risks, and every risk has transfer value. Any risk you take in any aspect of your life prepares you take more and bigger risks in other parts of your life.

Several years ago Elizabeth was asked to teach storytelling at a conference called "The Arts in Religion and Community." Margie Brown agreed to teach fire-eating. It was not a planned part of the program, but there was much enthusiasm for such a class. Several people got up before dawn everyday to learn to eat fire. Most of them were middle-aged women who were attending the conference because they were involved in clown ministry through their churches. Every morning the conversation in Elizabeth's group would be something like, "I talked to my husband, Larry, last night. He was horrified when I told him I was coming to this fire-eating class. He absolutely refused to allow me to come to this class again! Would you pass that fuel over here to me when you are finished with it?"

You could tell that the woman speaking had begun to understand the transfer value of taking risks. You also knew that the woman was not going to return home the same individual who left just a few days ago. You also knew husband Larry was in for some rocky times if he expected things to stay the same.

Every day we face fears. Every day we deal with things that would scare the socks off a sensible person. But as artists we are called to work at our art and doing so makes demands on us. It makes demands on our time ("How will I have the time to do this and where will I tell it?"). It makes demands on us to take risks. It makes demands on us to feel stupid or unappreciated. The end result is well worth all that effort.

We are not telling you not to be fearful. Fear is actually useful. It protects us. A child who has gotten burned knows to be careful of the stove. We always need to examine our fears and ask ourselves, "Do I still need this? Does it still serve me?" Being afraid of the stove is a good thing. Being so afraid of the stove that you cannot put dinner in the oven is not a good thing.

An artist is prepared to be fearless in the service of his art. Do you really have a right to your fear? Does it serve or hinder you? If you are an artist, is your fear so important to you that you would let it keep you from doing your right work? From giving the community those things which you are best qualified to do?

Understand this from your beating heart to your bones: that which calls out to be spoken by you has no voice but yours.

Suggested Further Reading

Orland, Ted, and David Bayles. *Art and Fear: Observations On the Perils (and Rewards) of Artmaking*. Santa Barbara: Capra Press, 1993.

May, Rollo. *The Courage to Create*. New York: W.W. Norton, 1975.

What are the specific reasons why you do not tell difficult stories?

Fear is a shape-shifter. It may shape itself in many ways. Are these your reasons?

- "I do not want to hurt anyone's feelings."
- "My family does not want their dirty linen washed in public."
- "No one wants to hear about my experiences."

It is important to get in touch with the fear that lies beneath these statements. To do this, write about each of the reasons that causes you to hesitate. It may be helpful to write about them in this format:

"I am afraid that _____."

or

"I am afraid _____."

Take your time in the writing. Give yourself the opp r-tunity to be with each of your fears as they surface.)o not dismiss any of them as being silly or inconsequ 1-tial. Write about what each of them means to you If you fail to take time to do this, one of these fears is lil ly to sabotage you when you least expect it.

Look at what you have written. The ones you wrote st are the ones that sit on the surface. There may be a dee er fear that lies at the heart of all the others. Maybe th re was one that bubbled up that made you go, "Ohhh! If you did not write it down, do so now. Go after it. N 1e it. Ancient wisdom is filled with stories that teach is that naming something gives us power over it.

A Consideration of Some Basic Principles

Whatever you put your trust in
can be the precipitating agent for your cure.
—Dr. Irving Oyle

Three basic principles make up the foundation for the telling of difficult stories: Trust, Permission, and Ownership. Like a three-legged stool, each principle supports the others. Without their working in concert to support the weight, the stool wobbles. Underlying the decision to tell difficult stories is an understanding that these principles must work together to make these stories both authentic and effective.

The relationship of the storyteller and the listener is much like that of tourist and tour guide. The storyteller offers to take you on a journey, to show you some interesting sights and some fascinating people. Included in that is the implicit agreement that she will bring you safely home. If a tour guide takes you to some dark and scary place, then abandons you to find your own way back, you have every right to be upset. By the same token, a storyteller who invites you to go with her into the story and becomes lost or too emotional to go on has abdicated her responsibility to the listeners. By building our stories upon the foundation of these principles, we can feel a lot more confident that those we take into the wilderness will be able to return.

— Trust

The first principle is trust. Do you trust yourself enough to be honest about the material? Will you shape it to make clear what happened and what it means? Do you trust the listener enough to share stories that might be discomforting to them or potentially embarrassing to you? Do you trust the story to be meaningful and interesting? Could it be told by another? Would you trust another teller enough to let him tell your story?

To acknowledge the listeners' trust, your relationship to the choices you make in telling a difficult story must be clear to yourself and to them. That is not to say that it must always be easy or obvious to the listener. But you must be willing to take responsibility for every choice you have made in the story.

The listener must trust you before she is willing to listen to the story you wish to tell. Building a relationship of trust is essential to the success of the experience. You cannot force anyone to listen. Most adults have developed effective ways of stopping their ears to that which they do not wish to hear.

This first diagram illustrates the relationship of the storyteller to the story and to the listener. The storyteller has a relationship

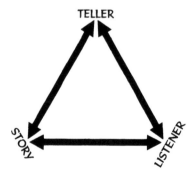

first to the story itself, and then to the listener. The focus of the first relationship is to enable the teller to share a personally meaningful story with the listener, so that the listener can in turn develop a direct relationship with the story itself.

Into this equation we can now insert the basic princ les of trust, permission, and ownership.

We should note here that for each of the relationship there are multiple and repeated connections. The three princip s play a role along each side of the triangle. There are elements trust between teller and story, between teller and listener, between listener and story. Similarly, there are multiple relationships operating for permission and ownership. So one way to think about it is that each arrow in the diagram expresses a three-part relationship—namely, that of permission, trust, and ownership—in relation to story, teller, and listener.

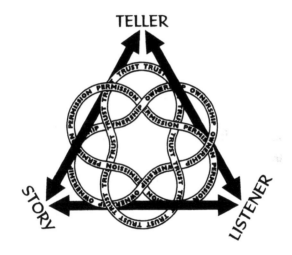

Of course you want to tell the stories that move you. If they do not move you, they cannot move your listeners. It is impossible to give away what you do not have. If, however, the story moves you beyond your level of control, the listener stops focusing on the story. You, and not the story, become the focus of the listener's attention.

One does not have to think of oneself as a storyteller to see this dynamic in action. Lawyers, ministers, and others who tell difficult stories within their work must be mindful of this as well.

A breach of this nature can have a severe and long-lasting effect on their relationships with those they serve.

── Permission ───────────────────

Here are fundamental questions to ask about permission: have you given yourself permission to tell this story? Have you accepted the risk that your listeners may view you differently if they hear this story? Do you have the permission of the other people in the story to tell this story about them? If not, are you willing to make sufficient changes in the story to protect their identity? Do you have your listeners' permission to tell this specific story now? (We would again point out that some stories are well suited for one kind of listener in a particular circumstance but not necessarily appropriate in another.)

One fundamental way to gauge whether you have the listeners' permission to tell is by actually listening to *them* and observing their behavior. Are they attentive or shuffling in their seats? How many of them will forego politeness and head for the exits once they realize that you are telling a discomforting tale? If you do not have tacit permission to tell them a difficult story, you should not be surprised if they do bolt.

Ask yourself, how have you prepared the listener to hear this material? If there is language or subject matter that might offend, do you provide a content warning? A content warning need not be elaborate, but it should be clear. It can be as simple as, "The story I am about to tell deals with [X], and those who may be offended may leave the room now. Those who choose to stay should be aware that this is a story in which language and situations may have a sharper edge than what you may usually hear in stories."

Is the material introduced in a way that makes clear the reason you're telling this story and gives the listener a reason to listen to the story? Are you prepared to talk about the content (your choice to tell it afterwards? If you are not, perhaps you ould forgo the experience.

Elizabeth often uses an effective formula for moving a audience through increasingly difficult stories: *Haha* (hur)r)—*Ahha* (wonder)—*Ahh* (understanding)—*Amen* (resolutior If at any point she senses that the audience is not prepared t make the next step she can stay where she is or go back to the p vious level of comfort and try again. Loren often groups stories ound central themes, and by working through variations on the reme can tell stories with subject matters and points of view that ill be accepted because of their relationship to what else has bee told.

We cannot stress enough the need for "honesty" in tell g difficult stories. You can't ask your listeners to fully enter th story if you are not prepared to enter it as well. That means tl t you must have made conscious decisions about what the story s and how you are going to tell it. You must have come to terms with your own discomfort with the subject matter and be prepared to own the story.

—Ownership

When we say that we "own" a story, we mean that we have internalized it. We are comfortable with it. We know what it is about and what it means, at least for us. To own a story means it has passed from the realm of something we have memorized into something we know so well that we can tell it in our own words and be faithful to the spirit and meaning of the tale. We know more than we tell.

The value of ownership is that it gives us confidence and choice. This is true whether the material is a traditional story or a personal narrative.

In some storytelling circles there is concern about issues of copyright and usage. When is a story mine? Who needs to ask permission and for what? From a technical point of view, copyright does not protect the idea, plot, or characters of a story but the specific expression of those constructs. In our discussion of ownership, we are not primarily concerned about issues of copyright, but we want to acknowledge that there are both ethical and legal considerations that we will not address here.

We do want to suggest, however, that when a story is truly owned, the unique language and style of the teller will be deeply impressed upon it. It is such ownership of a story that distinguishes one teller's version of a traditional tale from another's.

Let's look back to the diagram again. Ownership is where we reward the listener's trust and permission with our responsibility to make the telling honest and artful. The well-told story invites the listener to imaginatively enter the story and ultimately, to own it for themselves.

Pick a story that you tell and write out the following:

- What are the elements of trust (for yourself and listeners) that are necessary to tell it?

- When can it be told?

- To which audiences or in what circumstances?

- What are the elements of permission in those relationships?

- In what ways do you own it?

- What language or images are specific to your understanding and sharing of this story?

FOUR

Traditional Stories

A myth is a public dream, and a dream is a private myth.
—Joseph Campbell

People who believe the folktale is harmless are misinformed. For thousands of years people—not their leaders—told stories to inspire and inform, to infuriate and to challenge. The elderly men and women who sat by the fire day after day watched the interactions of the people around them. They used what they observed and their own imaginations to create stories. What they created was high art.

The grandmother could sit by the fire and spin a story to tell her granddaughters what they needed to know. She could tell the story in front of the family perpetrator. He would nod and smile to hear the story unfold. Yet every female in the room would understand what was being said. The grandmother could not speak of her experience directly. She was beholden to the abuser for the roof over her head and the food in her mouth. Still she would find a way to speak the truth. That is the power of art.

A literary story is the product of one individual. It gives us one person's talent and their wisdom. The traditional story is the product of a whole chain of tellers. It gives us the distilled wisdom of the culture from which it springs, filtered over many years of telling and retelling. Examine a traditional story and you can see the values of the culture that told it. The story is shaped by the culture, and, in turn, the culture is shaped by the story.

Unlike real life, in the traditional story good and evil are easy to identify. The characters are broadly drawn. Often they do not have individual names; when they do, they tend to be names common to the cultures so that everyone can relate to them. The stories deal with themes, like death or evil, that reach across cultures and generations. These themes are presented in metaphor, speak to the heart, engage the imagination, and have lasting universal meaning.

The Brothers Grimm collected some 385 stories. How many of them do we still hear told? Our culture wants to soften them, to rid them of all their hard edges and their hard truths. When we tell only the sanitized versions, we may say the story is still told but it does not do its true work.

Nearly every child in America can tell you the story of Cinderella. Some of them have watched the Disney version of the movie so often they can recite the dialogue. By the time they are old enough for the story of Cinderella to be of real emotional help to them, they have heard it so often they are deaf to it. Middle school girls think it is a "baby story." It would be of great value to them to hear the old version in which the stepsisters cut off their toes and heels to try to make the shoe fit, since metaphorically they are asked to do that in the name of fashion everyday.

There are people who want to water down the old tales. Bruno Bettelheim called them "the fairy tales baiters." They want to strip the traditional stories of all violence. Even those who are truly evil must be kindly dealt with. They wish to round off all the sharp points and soften the truths that give the stories their power. Making pablum of the stories serves no one. They become too anemic to perform the function for which they were intended: to clarify the real moral issues and choices we face. Children can easily think in metaphor. They understand that the "wicked stepmother" is not their father's second wife. They understand that the person being discussed is their own mother when she is being her witch-self. Children know what that is like, some more than others.

Here is a story to illustrate what we mean by a "traditional" tale fortified with its hard edges and potent meaning.

ELIZABETH ELLIS

Mister Fox

I grew up in the Appalachian Mountains hearing lots of stories. My aunt, Ida Gabbard Moore, loved to tell the old tales. This is the Bluebeard tale "Mister Fox," the way she always told it, incorporating her dialect and speech patterns.

Polly's family was dead, so she lived by herself in the settlement. When she was a young woman, fully grown, a stranger came into the territory. He cut quite a figure with his tall black boots and his fine black hat. Polly was pretty, so no one was surprised when he started calling on her.

At first Polly was pleased with his attention. After while, she began to think that he was strange. He never would talk about where he came from or who his people were. He said he had a big fine house up in the woods. Polly thought if it was as fine as he said it was, he'd invite a lot of company, but nobody had ever been there.

One day Mister Fox said, "This coming Saturday evening at sundown, I want you to meet me up on the ridge by that big old pine tree." Polly said she would, but after Mister Fox left she got to studying about that. It seemed strange that he would ask her to meet him in such a lonesome, out-of-the-way place. Polly wasn't sure she liked the idea much.

When Saturday arrived, it was cold with a bitter wind blowing. At first Polly started to stay at home. A woman who had been a friend of her mother's lived in the last house as you went out the ridge from the settlement. Polly had not seen her in some time, so she decided to leave early and stop off to have a good long talk with her mother's friend.

When she got there, nobody was home. She sat on the front porch for awhile. Finally she decided they must be gone for the day, so she started on out the ridge. It didn't take her long to get to that pine tree. She sat on a rock and waited for Mister Fox. The wind was blowing even colder that high up, and there wasn't anything around to break that wind. Polly looked up in that pine tree. It seemed like it would be a lot warmer up there out of the wind, so Polly climbed up into the tree branches.

She had been sitting up in there for sometime when she noticed Mister Fox coming out the ridge. He was a lot earlier than he had said that they should meet. Polly thought that was strange. He kept looking back over his shoulder, down toward the settlement. That seemed so odd she did not call out to him. Instead, she watched to see what he would do.

He went some little distance away from the tree. Polly watched as he pulled a mattock and a shovel out of the weeds. She could see he was digging a hole. Polly scooted over on the branch so she could get a better look. Now she could see that it was about six feet long and about three feet wide and a sight how deep. She knew then it was a grave.

She knew it was for her.

She sat on that branch as still as a stone. Mister Fox dug hard and deep for awhile. Then he began to dig more owly. Every minute or two he would stop and look off down the ridge. Finally, about sundown, he hid the mattock and shovel in the weeds and sat down underneath the tree. Polly was so scared he would look up in the branches and see her there. But he kept looking down the ridge toward the settlement. He sat there till it got hard dark. Then he swore an awful oath and walked off. Polly eased down out of the tree and started for home. She didn't go by the road for fear of Mister Fox. Instead, she took to the weeds and the bushes. When she got home her face and legs were all scratched and her dress was torn, but she was still alive.

The next time Mister Fox came to visit, he asked her why she had not come to meet him like she said she would. Polly said, "I was feeling poorly, and it was too cold to go out."

Mister Fox said, "I want you to come to my house and visit me." Polly asked, "When do you want me to come?" He said, "Sunday. That's a good day for a visit." She said all right, she'd come. A little later, she said, "I made a dried apple cake today. Do you want to try some?" Mister Fox said that sounded good. Polly went to the kitchen, built up the fire in the stove, and put on a pot of coffee. She peeked in at Mister Fox. He was sitting, looking into the fireplace.

Polly got a little poke and filled it with some cornmeal. She eased open the back door. She slipped around the side of the house and tied that little poke of cornmeal to the tail of Mister Fox's horse and slipped back inside.

The next morning, Polly got up early and dressed up warm. She started back up the ridge, following that trail of cornmeal. The wind had blown some of it away. Some places the birds had come to it. But any time she would be about to give up, she would see some of it a little further on.

She followed it into the deep woods, and after a while she spotted the top of a two-story cabin. She hid herself in the brush, and before too long Mister Fox came out the door. He got on his horse and rode off. Polly walked up to the front of the house and onto the porch. Just as she put her hand on the latch, she heard a voice say, "Be bold." She was startled, but it didn't sound like a human voice, so Polly went in.

On the table in front of her was a large cage, and in it was a parrot. She said, "You're a pretty bird." The parrot said, "Be bold, be bold." So Polly started looking around. It looked like any other house where a man had been living alone, kind of messy. Then she noticed the stairs going up to the second floor. Just as she put her foot on the bottom step, the parrot said, "Be bold. Be bold, but not too bold." Polly climbed up to the landing. There were two doors. She opened the one on the right. It was an ordinary bedroom. She moved to the door on the left. Just as she touched the latch, the bird said, "Be bold. Be bold, but not too bold, lest your heart's blood run cold."

When the door swung open, before her was a pure slaughterhouse. The walls and floor were spattered with blood. The bodies of young women hung from hooks on the wall. She saw barrels of blood and boxes of bones and hanks of hair. Polly screamed and slammed the door. She ran down the steps. Just as she reached the bottom, she heard the sound of a horse outside. She said to the parrot, "Polly, pretty Polly, don't tell no tales on me." The bird was silent.

Polly looked frantically around for a place to hide. She dove under the stairs and hid among the trunks and boxes that were stored there. Mister Fox threw open the door. He was dragging a young woman by the arm. She was shrieki g and struggling to free herself. Mister Fox drew back his a and slapped her across the face. The young woman grew qu t. He spoke to the parrot, "Has anybody been here while I' been gone?" Polly held her breath, but the bird said, "No, r."

Mister Fox began dragging the young woman the steps. It seemed like she roused herself a little, for she g bbed onto the railing and would not let go. Mister Fox stt ggled with her a while, but he lost his patience. He pulled it his sword and hacked off the woman's hand.

The hand fell right through the wooden slats and nded in Polly's lap. She clapped her hand to her mouth keep from screaming. When she heard the slaughterhou door slam shut, she knew there was nothing she could do help that poor young woman.

The parrot said, "Run, Polly, run." So Polly dashed out the door. She jumped on the horse tied outside and did not stop till she was safely home. She dismounted and gave the horse a slap across the rump to send it back to Mister Fox's house.

The next day was Saturday. There was to be a dance in the settlement that night. Polly saw Mister Fox, but she made her excuses not to dance with him. Everybody had a good time till the fiddlers got tired. While they were taking a rest, the young people gathered around the fireplace with the old folks and Polly. They began to tell stories and ask riddles. When it came to Polly, she said she had a riddle. They asked her to tell it.

She said:

"I was high and he was low.
The tree did shake. The wind did blow.

How I cried and my heart ached
to see the hole a fox did make."

Some of them tried to guess the meaning, but no one could. Polly said, "I'll tell you the answer directly." She saw Mister Fox had a worried look on his face.

So the stories and the riddles went round again. When they came to Polly, she said she did not have another riddle.

"I had a dream," she said. "Do you want me to tell it to you?"

Mister Fox said, "Huh! There's nothing to dreams." But everybody else urged Polly to tell it.

She said, "I dreamed I went way out on the ridge and back in the woods. I came to a big old two-story cabin. I dreamed Mister Fox came out and rode away." Polly saw all the color drain out of Mister Fox's face.

She said, "I dreamed I started to open the door. I heard a voice say, 'Be bold. Be bold.' I went in and saw a parrot in a cage."

Mister Fox said, "It is not so. It was not so."

Polly continued, "I dreamed I started to go up the stairs. The parrot said, 'Be bold. Be bold, but not too bold.'"

Mister Fox said, "It is not so. It was not so."

Polly kept on, "I dreamed I came to a door. The bird said, 'Be bold. Be bold, but not too bold, lest your heart's blood run cold.'"

Mister Fox said, "It is not so. It was not so."

Polly said, "I dreamed I opened the door, and it looked like a smokehouse, only it was women hanging instead of meat."

Mister Fox said, "It is not so. It was not so. And God forbid it should be so."

Polly said, "I ran down the stairs, and Mister Fox arrived dragging a young woman behind him. When she grabbed the railing to try to save herself, he pulled out his sword and hacked off her hand."

Mister Fox cried out, "It is not so. It was not so. And God forbid it should be so."

Polly jumped to her feet and called out, "It is so, and it was so. And here's the bloody hand to show." She drew the hand from her pocket and threw it on the ground at Mister Fox's feet.

The men of that settlement, young and old, took hold of Mister Fox and brought him to the high sheriff. And it wasn't long before he was hanged.

Like the stories collected by the Brothers Grimm and many tales from other ethnic traditions, there is a sense of justice in this tale. It is metaphoric and in the application of justice not only does the punishment fit the crime, it speaks with resonance to the issue.

When we speak of traditional story, we are also including myth. Think of stories such as *Oedipus* or *Beowulf*. Myth operates on an even more profound level than ordinary metaphor. It speaks to core values and time-tested truths of the culture. What is the answer to the riddle of humanity? How do we answer the summons of Fate or the requirement of duty? In *Beowulf*, as an example, the fundamental understanding of what it means to be a hero is delineated, both as deeds done and as obligations accepted. We could draw a direct line from the hero in that tale to John Wayne's principled cowboys or Clint Eastwood's iconic drifters.

Although the stories are often thick and complicated, it is worth examining them. Inside their character-rich texts are incidents and imagery we can share with others. They were the original soap operas and situation comedies. They both inspired and instructed generations about what was worth living and dying for. Their themes echo in all other traditional material and in the stories of our own lives.

The Gift and Shadow of —"Modern" Retellings

Often we think we know the old stories, and yet fail to see how they continue to speak to our experience. Sometimes we are so familiar with a story, or think we are, that we hear it as a kind of shorthand. When that is the case, one way to really let it into our psychic house is to give it new words. To tell something that begins with our everyday world and leads us into the terror and beauty of the old stories is both a gift and an adventure.

The risk of dressing the old stories in modern language is that we may not pay sufficient attention to the small details within the old structure. Or, in the age of political correctness, we may not pay attention to the shadow. However, the value of putting old stories into a modern context is that it lets us, or makes us, think through what they must do to reach our heart.

When we reframe an old story we need to think carefully about what it is and what it means. Can we substitute what is familiar to ourselves and our listeners for the general details and settings of the old? Are the themes and characters suitable for retelling? To make it relevant, it is not a matter of ripping the darkness from the woods but to make sure that the listener can still see the shape of the forest behind the newly planted trees. Can we feel the temperature drop in the pine shadows and the warmth of the sunlight even as we take a new path to a familiar destination? Can we recognize the stepmother or the witch, the fool or the king, if they go by another name?

Here is a story to illustrate what we mean by a "modern retelling."

—————————————————————LOREN NIEMI—

Hansel and Gretel

Once there was a man who carried a large stone upon his back. One day his son asked, Father, why are you carrying that heavy burden?

The old man said, It is tradition. My father did it and his father before him. Someday, son, you will have this duty as well.

The boy felt such pity for the father's pain that he could hardly wait to grow up so he could carry the rock. Eventually he did, and when the father passed the burden from his shoulder to the boy's the most amazing thing happened.

The old man straightened up. He began to rise. His feet left the ground and he floated into the sky. Looking down, he said, Goodbye, son.

Goodbye, father.

Now the boy carried the weight and soon became quite used to it. Then he met an attractive woman who asked Why are you carrying that stone?

Tradition. My father did it and his father before him.

Drop that rock, she said, placing her hand on his cheek. I have something better for you to do.

When he let go of the stone to follow her into the house, it crashed to the ground and broke into a hundred pieces. Each one was a small white pebble.

· · ·

Once there lived a brother and a sister. Dutiful children, they did their chores without complaint and ate what little they were offered with gratitude. They lived with their poor father and stepmother at the edge of the dark tangle that was the forest. They were each other's sole companion.

That day the children were taken by their father into the woods to search for wild mushrooms. Sit here and wait for me, he said, then slipped from sight.

Patient they were, but he did not come back. The wait seemed eternal. The girl began to worry that night would come before father did.

Brother, I want to go home, she said.

Look at this pebble, the boy said. I took pebbles enough for each pocket from beside the door and have spent all day looking for one as smooth and white as the moon. This is good, but it is not right, he said, as he threw it aside.

Now is not the time for stones, she said. How will we get home?

Now, dear Sister, is precisely the time for stones. See, here is one that I discarded. And there, another. I'll bet I can find every one I have dropped and they will take us back to hearth and kin.

And so it was.

Oh, Stepmother was surprised to see them standing there as small and forlorn as abandoned kittens. Father all the more when he came, saying, Disobedient children, where did you go? I thought I told you to wait for me to return. To bed without supper it should be, but there is so little to eat that we will all go to bed hungry even if we do eat. But in that moment, something turned the lock in Stepmother's heart and she fastened it tight. She knew what was hard, in fact, was best. They would be better off without. Without these needy mouths and growing bodies. Without the need for new shoes, without the whimpering, without the mess. Without these reminders of another woman's love.

• • •

Once there had been plenty. But the days of fat sausage, thick-crusted bread, and golden foaming beer gave way to days of stale bread and the measured glass. Then even the beer was gone. The porridge, once thick as mortar, thinned itself until the bottom of the bowl could be seen through it and even the mice had lost interest.

Only Sister had seen how Stepmother looked at Brother. How she came to the bath as he scraped the hard muscle of youth with the lye soap, and sat next to the tin, sponge in hand, laughing that he would soon be a handsome man. But this night Father had walked through the room, and Sister could see from the way his smile fell that a disturbing notion had planted itself and was bearing bitter fruit.

Overheard she did, the mother making her case Take these children out to the woods and leave them. They re old enough to fend for themselves. We can have other ours. Overheard she did, Father asking what Stepmother ha been doing with the boy and cut off her stammered reply t agree that he would go looking for mushrooms tomorrow They were of one mind. Sister lay in her bed waiting for the cock's greeting with tears so spent they were distant memo

One small crust of bread was all any of them migl have. Sister ate hers, silently, without tasting it. Father wiped tl gruel pot with his and swallowed whole. Stepmother had n hing, but sat looking strangely at the boy. Brother saw Stepn ther's look, blushed, and left the table with bread still in h d.

Once more into the wood. Once more to wait for ther's promised return. Once more to know that he wou not.

Brother offered a trail of bread crumbs as if that would lead them to safety, but it only led to a bird, and another, and a squirrel working the hard crust as earnestly as any nut. Defeated by habit, what direction now, he wanted to know? What trail? It made no difference to her. Why bother going back? There was no welcome there.

· · ·

Once there lived a woman who in another time or place might have been called wise, or crone, or helpmate, but because she lived by herself at a distance, she was called witch. She tended that which must be done, cooked and baked, filled her time perfecting the arts and decorating for her pleasure, if no one else's.

Only a trick of the light let them see the tidy cottage nestled in the glade. Or an errant breeze that brought the smell of the oven, yeast bread made with yellow cream butter and glazed with a swirl of white sugar. His hunger complete, he did not knock or ask or listen to his sister's warning that it was theft. He simply took the smallest loaf and sat beneath the pink-trimmed shutters to have his fill.

It's better buttered and on a plate, a voice said. Manners and presentation, don't forget your manners and presentation, young man. They looked up to see the white-pressed apron and the pale lipstick smile. Martha, she said. You may call me Martha.

Ate they did until they could eat no more. All the time, the woman studied the girl as if taking her measure for a dress that was not yet made, or as if casting her for a part in a play that had not yet been written.

One night the girl thought that this one was better than Stepmother had ever been. She listened. She taught her things. How to bake and decorate. Gave her makeup tips. Combed and curled her long locks. Dressed her in smart little outfits. This one had big plans for her. This one knew what was best. Was proud of her. Wanted her success. Was the mother she deserved and had never had.

One night she wondered where Brother was. She had almost forgotten him. He had been there and . . . was he gone? Had he left without her? No, not likely. He ate too well, too often, to leave this banquet table. So she got up and looked in the dark corners and under the bed. She found him in the closet but the door would not open.

Gretel, is that you?

Yes, Hansel, come out.

I can't. She says it's for my own good, but there is nothing to do here but eat and wonder.

Wonder, indeed. Gretel told her brother to be brave, she would help.

How?

She did not know yet, but she would help all the time.

· · ·

Once there was an oven. Round as a beehive, large enough for ten loaves, the bricks fit snug. Once there was an oven that sang a song of ashes. That which would nourish must change. It sang the fire and sang the heat, sang the bread brown and the iron door shut. Come, it cried, come to me and you shall be transformed.

Oh, sweet one, prepare the oven. We have work to do. I cannot wait for the boy to grow a day plumper. He will have to do, and we will be better off without. Without his needy mouth and growing body. Without the lazy bones, without whimpering, and without the mess. And so Gretel went to stoke the fire and form a plan. But there was none, or perhaps, there was only one. A terrible deed that must be done. One would have to be lost and one saved, and she must decide which it would be.

Oh, Martha, I am unsure and in need of your counsel. Is this fire hot enough? Come look, and tell me true.

Once there was an oven. Round as a beehive, the bricks fit snug. It sang the fire and sang the heat, sang the ashes and the iron door. A push was all it took. And when it was full, the smoke rose dark. It hung in the trees and filled the woods with the smell of burnt meat, burnt bones. Come, it cried, come to me and you shall be transformed.

. . .

Oh, how shall we end this tale? What would comfort you? Shall we have them climb on the back of ducks to cross the lake? Go home and find Stepmother conveniently gone and Father repentant? Shall we have them stay in the little cottage and live off the spoils of death? Shall we have them wander the world in search of princes or queens? Or shall we say that they made one choice and then made another, and the best we can hope for is that in the end they loved and cared for one another?

The old stories carried a power to compress the complexities of experience and engage the imagination. They used powerful imagery and simple narrative forms to carry deeply felt psychological truths. They still can serve that function. King Midas still speaks to a dot-com reality. The essential message of the story— be careful what you wish for or be prepared to take up your burden to right the world turned upside-down—resonates as strongly now as it ever has. Perhaps more so.

There is also a value in looking at the stories not often told to see what is there. How many people are familiar with the Brothers Grimm's version of "Bearskin," with its roots in anti-war sentiment? How many have read Italio Calvino's wonderful collection of Italian folktales, which includes a version of "Sleeping Beauty" where it is not a kiss but the act of giving birth that wakes her from her adolescent slumber?

For mass American culture, the traditional stories we know are largely from the Western European tradition. Yet every culture has a store of folktales to explain, warn, and guide us through the thicket of folly. What rich tales that speak to our troubled times from which ethnic and religious traditions are waiting to be shared?

The old stories, both myth and folktale, have great power. Metaphorically, they speak to us of issues with which we struggle every day.

During the last few months, the two of us have struggled with maintaining our busy schedules of performances and workshops, family responsibilities, and board or committee assignments, in addition to preparing this manuscript for publication. One of the old tales that has come to mind again and again is the story of Sisyphus, endlessly rolling the stone up the hill, only to have it roll down again so the everlasting job can be started anew.

What story are you currently living? What story is living you?

Ethnic and religious traditions around the globe have bequeathed us rich tales that still speak to our troubled times. Hundreds of them are waiting to be shared. Begin with the stories of your own culture, but do not stop there. Look beyond the obvious. Seek out variants of well-worn tales so they can be heard with new ears. Here are some popular images from mythology—

- Atlas holding up the world
- Hercules cleaning out the stables
- Odysseus coming home

or some from well-known folktales—

- Cinderella sitting in the ashes
- Sleeping Beauty waiting to be awakened
- Prince Charming, the rescuer, in the thornbushes

Identify one of the old tales that resonates with your life. Think with your heart, not your head. Then take some time to journal about the images of that old story and what they mean to you. You may be surprised by the insight you gain about your life.

Historical Stories

*The history of an oppressed people is hidden in the es
and the agreed upon myth of its conquerors.*
—Meridel LeSuer

To work with historical story, you must deal with the issue of
"political correctness." To us, the term "politically correct" is an
oxymoronic expression—like "jumbo shrimp," "military intel-
ligence," or "limited nuclear war." That which is political is
rarely correct; and that which is correct is rarely political.

The problem with "political correctness" is it presumes that
someone's politics are "correct." This idea directly opposes the concept that human beings embrace politics out of necessity, not out
of choice, to keep each other in balance. That which is thought
of as being "politically correct" changes according to time, gender, culture, and ethnicity, as rapidly as the newest fashion trend
or hit TV show comes and goes.

When we began developing a workshop on the telling of difficult stories, we called it "Telling the Darkness" as a reference to
the shadow side of human experience. When we presented it at
the National Storytelling Conference in San Diego, it was suggested that associating difficult stories with darkness could be
offensive to people of color. We were not so wedded to the title

that we could not change it. So when asked to present a longer version at the National Storytelling Conference in Kingsport, Tennessee, we called it "Telling the Difficult." What we lost in poetic imagery, we gained in unaffected directness.

The first time we shared the title of this book with colleagues, we were again taken to task, this time for disparaging wolves. We acknowledge that the wolf, as symbol and as creature, has suffered mightily. However, we think when you invite the wolf in, you do not denigrate him. If anything, we rejoice in his company and hope that in the course of this text we can come to a new appreciation of his role in the psychological landscape.

Political correctness is often a popular form of censorship. We do not choose to let it dictate the stories that we tell or how we tell them. When we bow before that altar, we turn our backs on authentic story. When political correctness motivates us, we give up our genuine voice.

While we may not be interested in being "politically correct," we have devoted our lives to being ethical individuals. We have no desire to inflict unnecessary pain on anyone. If any act on our part is hurtful to someone else, we want to consider it carefully. Each of us has been in situations where others were offended by what we chose to say or do. When that happens, we feel it is necessary to listen very carefully to what is being said. Often that is more difficult than it sounds, especially if we feel attacked.

Listening carefully is the only way to learn what is really at the heart of the matter. Perhaps the person challenging us has a valid point to make. He may see things of which we have been unaware. There could be hidden cultural meanings about which we need to be educated.

It is also possible that the problem is not ours, but someone else's. It may be that their issue is theirs alone and we cannot and should not take it as ours. We may be dealing with a person who was wounded in another situation. We may be receiving the fallout from a problem we had nothing to do with. There only one way to reach clarity about the situation: reserve judgment and listen carefully.

Give up seeking "easy answers." That's another one of those oxymoronic expressions. If it is easy, it probably isn't the answer. If it is the answer, it probably won't be easy. These two poles of political correctness and ethical behavior, with their inherent contradictions, are the paradox with which we grapple every day. Continually wrestling with this incongruity gives our stories power and purpose. A similar struggle lies before you.

Nowhere is this labor more evident than when we come to dealing with historical texts. Here all the conflicting needs of honesty and collective denial of political correctness come to bear. The presentation of one side of the story is sure to gore someone's ox. The telling of multiple sides of the story, unless done carefully, may lead to confusion. It is in the presentation of difficult stories based on historical texts that we most need to be clear about what it is we want to say and why we want to say it.

To create a story from historical material, you will need to look at the two types of sources: primary documents and secondary ones. A primary historical document, such as a letter or a journal entry, comes from someone immediately involved in the event under consideration. The Declaration of Independence is a primary source document. So are the letters that passed between Abigail Adams and her husband, John, while the Declaration was being written. Even a newspaper account of the signing of the document, written at the time of the signing, is now a primary document.

A secondary source may be true and accurate, but it is removed from the event by space or time. A history of the pivotal documents that changed the world would be a secondary source, as would a biography of Abigail Adams written in our time.

As a starting point for the creation of effective historical stories, each type of historical material has its strengths. Primary material gives you the voice of the people actually having the experience. It has their emotion and their insights. Secondary material helps us see the situation in perspective. It gives us a "bigger" picture. Each of these types has its weakness as well. The secondary source alone may be dry and unmoving. Or it may reflect a particular contemporary bias that does a disservice to our understanding of the subject. Viewed in isolation, the primary source may lack scope. It may be ignorant of the complexities of time or culture. The soldier in the foxhole knows the fear and the blood. His letter home is a primary source that helps us understand what it is like to be there. He does not, however, know the lasting significance of the battle in which he is engaged. For that we must turn to secondary sources. The two taken together give us a more complete picture of the event being examined.

There is much in primary historical source material that will shock and offend contemporary listeners. It is filled with the vilest racism. Sexism pervades every page. Dealing with this material is not for sissies. It takes courage to examine the material closely and get in touch with the world view it represents. It takes wisdom to decide which parts of it to bring to your listeners.

There is a great deal of pressure for political correctness. It is popular to whitewash stories from the past to make things appear much better than they actually were for many people. Those who fall into this trap are often motivated by misplaced kindness. They do not want to hurt anyone's feelings. They do not wish to offend. They do not want to feel guilty.

There is little value in denying the reality of the cultural beliefs reflected in historical material. In fact, we would argue the necessity of "letting the warts show." When we do this w arrive at a clearer and more accurate presentation of the difficu than we can from trying to reshape it to meet our conventions what the world should look like. The pain of racism, sexis , and classism is better understood when it is directly presente than when we try to rewrite it.

We are all an American family. Being lied to about ou trou- bled childhood—that is to say, our family history—does n serve us. It renders us unable to understand our present situati 1 and makes us incapable of building a foundation of trust for the uture.

Here is a story to illustrate what we mean by a "hi orical story." It is shaped to bring a particular person to life an is set realistically in the time and place in which she lived.

—ELIZABETH E S—

Mary McLeod Bethune

The Ku Klux Klan sent word to Mary McLeod Bethune that she better not try to vote, but she said, "Women haven't had the vote long enough for me to let a bunch of men in bedsheets keep me away from the polls." So she went and cast her ballot.

Then they sent word to her that she better not try to edu- cate any more African-American children. When fall came, however, she got in her buggy and drove down every back road begging parents and grandparents to send their children to her school. When school opened, she had twice as many children enrolled as she had had the year before. So the Klan decided it was time to pay her a visit, as a warning to her and all the other "uppity niggers."

She was sitting at her desk one night, making out a test

for the next day's lesson, when a little boy came thundering into the room. She could tell he had been running a long way because he could hardly catch his breath. When he did, he gasped out, "They're coming!" She said, "Who's coming?", but she already knew the answer. He said, "Men with guns and clubs. My daddy says you can't be here when they get here."

She walked around the desk. She put her hand on the child's head and said, "You run home now. You tell your daddy I said thank you."

She knew that the little boy and his father lived on the state highway where the country road met it to run in front of her school. She also knew that the little boy's father had risked his life to send her that message.

She walked out into the main room of her school and began to pull on a rope attached to an old bell. She could hear footsteps running from every direction. There were so few schools for African-American students that the children lived too far away to go home at night. They stayed at school all week and went home on Friday if someone came with a mule to fetch them. The teachers lived too far away as well, and stayed there all week with the children.

When everyone was gathered, Mary McLeod Bethune said to them, "The Klan is on its way to pay us a visit."

There was a murmur of fear that swept through the room. Even the youngest of the children had heard about the beatings and the lynchings.

She said, "I want all you teachers to turn off all the lights." They nodded. She continued, "When I clap my hands for the signal, I want you to turn on all the lights at once."

One teacher asked her the only question: "Won't that make us a bigger target?"

"Just do as I ask," she begged.

The teachers fanned out around the school and all the lights went out. Now you could look out the darkened windows and see thirty or forty pairs of headlights coming down the road.

She turned to the children and said, "You little ones stay where you are and try not to be afraid. You older ones, you come with me. We will go and meet them. Whatever I do, you do it too."

They trusted her, so they followed her.

She stood on the bottom step of the school. The children arranged themselves on the stairs behind her. By now the motorcade had reached the end of her driveway. She stood and waited. The first car stopped. A man got out in a long white robe and a tall pointed cap. He had a mask across his face. In the glare of the headlights you could see the purple insignia of the Ku Klux Klan. He stood there and held the oncoming traffic back, so that the entire motorcade could pass down her driveway without being interrupted. Still she stood and waited.

When the headlights of the first car flashed across her body, she clapped her hands for the signal. Every light behind her came on at once. Standing there with that bright light shining in front of and behind her, she looked like some tall, dark avenging angel.

She opened her mouth and began to sing. It was an old song, born of her people's pain and their perseverance— *"When Israel was in Egypt land..."* And the children on the steps behind her answered back as they always did when that old song was sung, *"... Let my people go."*

That first car kept edging past them. Mary McLeod Bethune's voice grew stronger. The children sang louder. The cars just kept inching by them. The men in the cars began to hunker down in their seats like it had finally dawned on them what it meant for a bunch of men to come, armed with guns and clubs, after an old woman and a school full of children. Not one car stopped.

I wish I could tell you that Mary McLeod Bethune never had any more trouble with the Ku Klux Klan, but you and I both know that ignorance takes a long time to die.

Again it was after dark. Have you ever noticed that when you deal with cowards it is quite likely to be after dark? This time there was no messenger. She looked up from her desk to find that there was already a cross on the lawn, and it was already blazing.

She jumped up and ran out the door. She could see four white-robed figures climbing into the back of an old touring car, the forerunner of our modern-day convertibles. She didn't think about her own safety. All she thought about was her school. That old wood, the peeling paint: just a few sparks from that fire and everything she had worked for in her lifetime would be in ashes at her feet.

She was a huge woman with massive arms. She had picked many a pound of cotton in her childhood. She went running toward the cross. It was only burning at the top. She grabbed it up out of the ground. She swung it around her head and flung it as far as she could make it go. It tumbled end over end over end, and landed—in the back of the touring car.

Instantly, four men were screaming and rolling on the ground. Mary McLeod Bethune went running to help them. She had no desire to hurt them. She had only been trying to send that flame as far away from her old wooden building as she could make it go.

Up to that time, the Ku Klux Klan had a stranglehold on

Daytona, Florida. Their biggest weapon was secrecy. No matter how you felt about what they did, you'd never open your mouth. You never knew who you were speaking to. You didn't know if you were talking to a member of the Klan, or to a member of one of those old Klan families. So good people said nothing. We all know what happens when good people say nothing.

But after that, if you wanted to know who the leaders of the Klan were, all you had to do was look around town that week. They were the men wearing the bandages over their burns. People began to laugh behind their hands about a bunch of men who had been bested by an old fat woman. After people laugh at something it is never quite so strong again.

So the power of the Klan was broken there in Daytona, Florida. Mary McLeod Bethune's school has never closed. You could visit it today. It is called Bethune-Cookman College.

In working on this story, Elizabeth read books about life in the South, covering 1865 to 1950. She also read current biographies of Mary McLeod Bethune. These secondary sources were invaluable for understanding Mary McLeod Bethune's contribution to our history as a nation. Newspaper accounts from Daytona during the 1930s and the letters of Mary McLeod Bethune herself are the primary sources which give this story its voice.

Elizabeth's experience with telling this story is informative. She has been lambasted several times by listeners who say the story should not be told. They ask why she has to "open that can of worms again." She has been chastised for telling a story that "makes white people look bad." After listening carefully to their objections, she decided it is a powerful story with great relevance for our time, even if hearing it makes some people uncomfortable.

She has also been taken to task by some storytellers who say she has no right to tell it because she is not African-American. After painstaking consideration, Elizabeth decided to continue telling the story because she feels a deep connection with Mrs. Bethune and her love for children. She does not feel it is necessary to be African-American to revere Mrs. Bethune and wish to share her story with those who have not heard it. She does, however, believe that being African-American could increase the insight and understanding with which the story is shared. Toward that end, she is eager to share her research with anyone who also wants to tell it.

Neither of these decisions was reached without a great deal of soul searching. To do less would trivialize the story itself and corrode all future telling of it.

-isms of All Kinds

What happens when we let the language and world view which are found in those first sources show themselves for what they are? The problem with using "those words," with using another time or culture's point of view, is that it offends. People did speak with a careless disregard for feelings. People of color were not seen as equal or worthy of respect. There is in the historical source materials a casual racism about blacks and Asians that is so pervasive as to be unquestioned. The indigenous people were subject to the theft of their ancestral land and genocide. Succeeding generations of immigrants—the Irish, the Italians, the Poles, and Jews of every nationality—were the object of jokes and subject to institutional and economic prejudice.

Here is the fundamental problem: how can we deal with the difficult issues that historical texts present and not offend in the process? Our answer is that it may not be possible. When we do not tell the hard truth from the past, we are actively engaged in perpetuating a lie. To present the texts as they stand, without varnish or concern for political correctness, is what honesty requires. What we can and should do is prepare the listener for the offense by making clear who is speaking. This can be done in a brief introduction to the material or in the presentation contrasting views. To reach real understanding of an event or idea, we can, and often should, offer material that represent more than one point of view to let the competing human stories within the cultural framework be heard. A lengthy consideration of "point of view" will be given in chapter 7 and need not be presented here.

An effective story must have believable characters in it. In folktales, characters are often all good or all evil. This does not work when we are telling about people from real life. Presenting them in this way reduces them to flat cardboard cutouts instead of real flesh and blood. It makes their virtues and vices look smaller than they might actually have been and easier to disregard. Displaying them with both virtues and weaknesses highlighted helps us to invest ourselves in them.

Beware of the desire to give all the "good" characters modern sensibilities, and all the "bad" characters dated attitudes. Only characters perceived as real, and therefore a mixture of strengths and failings, can resonate with our listeners.

Tell of them in all their humanness. Thomas Jefferson was the main author of the Declaration of Independence; Thomas Jefferson was a slave owner. Any honest consideration of his life should include both of those facts.

The structuring of the historical story presents more challenges than any other type of narrative. Many elements of crafting that are germane to this type of work (such as the consideration of comedy or tragedy and point of entry considered in chapter 7 and of construction of emotional arc and moral framework in chapter 9) should be carefully considered and will prove quite useful.

Suggested Further Reading

The National Storytelling Association. *Many Voices: True Tales from America's Past.* Jonesborough, Tennessee: The National Storytelling Press, 1996.

Eisler, Riane. *The Chalice and the Blade.* San Francisco: HarperSanFrancisco, 1987.

Is a person a rebel or a patriot? The answer depends upon which side of the conflict you are on. If the person upholds the same philosophy as you do, you probably think of him as a partiot. If, however, he supports the other view, you probably think of him as a rebel.

The telling of all historical material is shaped by point of view. The story takes on the ideology of the character who is speaking. To understand the circumstances that formed any historical event, it is helpful to tell the story from more than one point of view. In fact, it is beneficial to our understanding if told from two conflicting points of view.

Choose one of your favorite historical events. Jot down some notes about what happened. Examine what you have written, and begin asking yourself why it happened. "Why" is always a much more interesting question than "what" or "how." Identify two opposing beliefs that are involved in the conflict that surrounds your chosen event.

Study the notes you made. How would someone on each side of this conflict interpret these facts? Tell the story of the event from the two opposing points of view. What is there to be learned from considering the voice of each position?

SIX

Emotional Timelines

Your vision will become clear
only when you can look into your own heart.
Who looks outside, dreams; who looks inside, awa_ s.
—Carl Jung

When we tell traditional stories, we know that we are hea ed off into the direction of "once upon a time." That is easy f(most people. The concept of telling stories from your own li! often seems more challenging. People say nothing interesting (excit-ing ever happened to them. They truly believe they have i thing to tell stories about.

They could not be more wrong. Within each of our l es are challenges and opportunities that have the potential o being great stories, worthy of all the comedy and drama we ha\ come to expect from traditional material.

Let's go back for a moment to the issue of what stories you are not telling and why. Sometimes we don't tell a story because we don't know where it really begins. Other times we don't know where it should end. There is often a tendency to tell too much, to fill in more action and detail than is really necessary for a tightly woven and inviting story.

Sometimes we don't tell the story because we haven't got a sense of its meaning. We think that the best way to achieve meaning is to just tell whatever is there. Consciously structuring the story means not only that you have to know what happens but, more importantly, knowing what you want to strip away. What you take out of the story may be as important as what you leave in.

We will look at these issues in more detail in the next chapter. The question before us now is how can we find the stories within our lives that are worth telling?

Emotional timelines can be quite helpful in showing us where this source material is hidden. Creating one for any emotion—anger, joy, wonder—will help identify lots of possible story material.

—Jealousy

Let's begin with the emotion of jealousy. It is an emotion most of us have experienced. Begin to think ugly green thoughts and try to get in touch with the times in your life when you have felt jealousy. If you were to make a timeline for yourself of your experience of that emotion, when and how often would jealousy appear? When have you felt wronged because you didn't have what you knew should be yours? Begin with early childhood, then look to later childhood, when you were a teen, when you were a young adult and when you were an adult. Trace the way it has manifested itself in your life.

For many of us, the birth of the new baby was our first experience of dealing with jealousy. Childhood is often filled with sibling rivalry. The teen years and young adult years are times for experiencing jealousy because of our relationships with members of the opposite sex. During these years we also begin to see others get the things we want. Adult years often bring us professional as well as personal jealousies.

If we were to create a table to help you identify when a l how
you have experienced jealousy, it would be arranged like t is:

Jealousy

Time of Life	What happened	Effect
EARLY CHILDHOOD		
LATER CHILDHOOD		
TEEN		
YOUNG ADULT		
ADULT		
WHATEVER'S NEXT		

At any point where you have experienced a strong er)tion,
no matter what that emotion may be, you have the se l of a
story. Most people share common feelings about the lives.
Something they can identify as having a strong emotiona harge
for them is quite likely to resonate with a great many oth   people who have felt similar emotions or lived similar situa   )ns.

Any time you have experienced a strong emotior bout
something or someone in your life you should treat it as green
shoot. You can work to understand it. Craft it and polis it for
telling as comedy or tragedy. A story about fighting wi your
brother or sister when you were children presents a bject
nearly everyone can understand. That could be a funny :)ry. It
does not have to be something painful to remind people   what
they have experienced.

For the 1999 National Storytelling Conference in San)iego,
the two of us decided we would use the emotional t eline
exercise and create new work based on it. As a theme, w chose
jealousy. The two stories that we developed for our works p are
quite different from one another, so both have been ir uded

here. Following each is a discussion of the process through which we shaped them.

ELIZABETH ELLIS —

Just Perfect

I guess I could have stood it if she had just been pretty. No, it wasn't that she was pretty. That would have been forgivable. She was perfect. She was pretty, but she was also smart and sweet and kind and good. There was absolutely nothing wrong with her. She was just perfect.

I met Helen Hackett the first day of my freshman year at college. She arrived early, and all her luggage matched. But she seemed to take great delight in helping those who arrived later lug their mismatched suitcases and cardboard boxes up three flights of stairs.

That evening, we all gathered in the parlor for an earnest talk by the Dean of Women. It was a religious college, so there was no shortage of rules to be discussed. At one point, while the dean was extolling the virtues of virtue, I glanced over at Helen Hackett. She rolled her eyes. The gesture should have endeared her to me and cemented our friendship, but it didn't. Somehow I hated that she had done that. It was just perfect.

The dean asked us to choose a representative to the Student Council. I had always been active in that in high school. I thought it would be great to continue doing it in college. I wanted the job, but I was too self-conscious to put myself forward. Before I knew it, Helen Hackett was appointed to the Student Council. As it turned out, she had a natural talent for leadership. I, on the other hand, had a natural talent for resentment.

A few days later, the Dean of Women caught me in dress that was far shorter than allowed. She said, "I want t make sure that you get off on the right foot here at co ge. I noticed yesterday that you did not wear heels and se to chapel. It has also come to my attention that you w e not appropriately dressed for dinner on Sunday evening.

Just then, Helen Hackett came tripping down tl steps beside us. "Look at her," said the dean. "Look at ho she is dressed. She is always just perfect!"

It only took me a couple of weeks to develop a h eless crush on my English professor. I had always thou ht of myself as a good writer. I was sure I would write an e y for him that would make him sit up and take notice. I rked extra hard on it, carefully selecting every word. I niled when I turned it in because I was sure it was my bes vork.

The next time the class met, the professor said, "I have received in this batch of essays the best student paper I have ever read." A thrill of pleasure ran through me. He continued, "It is by Helen Hackett, and I want to read it to you because it is just perfect."

That's the way it went throughout the year. I kept on schlepping along, and Helen Hackett kept on being perfect.

I stopped swooning over my English professor. Instead, for weeks I had cherished a secret crush on my lab partner, Phillip. He had the most beautiful blue eyes. I spent far more time watching them than I did looking at the Bunsen burners.

My roommate Susan said, "You've got to say something to him. You've got to make your move." I could not think of a single way to let him know how I felt. One evening Susan returned from the library with a giant grin on her face. "Your problem is solved," she told me. She handed me a flyer for the upcoming Sadie Hawkins Day Dance. "Girls ask the boys," she gloated. "It's just perfect."

She was right; it *was* just perfect. I would ask him to the dance and he would know that I wanted to be more than just a lab partner. Asking him, however, was heart-stoppingly scary. I dragged my feet for more than a week. Finally, Susan said, "Okay, today is the day! No backing out!"

That afternoon, standing by a bubbling beaker, I asked him if he would like to go to the dance with me. He said, "Gee, that would have been nice. But I already have a date. Helen Hackett asked me yesterday."

When Susan found me crying on my bed, she asked what was wrong. When I told her, she said, "Well, that's just perfect."

I decided to try out for a part in the spring play. I read well and was pretty sure that I would get a part. Maybe not a big part. After all, I was a freshman. But a part of some kind. It was late when Susan asked, "Well, did you get a part?"

"I don't know yet. The cast hasn't been posted."

"It has," Susan assured me. "Dottie was talking about it in the shower room."

Susan and I ran down the hall to Dottie's room to congratulate her. "Did you see my name on the list?" I asked her.

"Sorry," she said. "I was so excited about getting a part, I didn't think to look."

I was really frustrated because it was after curfew, so I would have to wait until tomorrow to find out.

Susan said, "Ask the housemother. Maybe she will let you run over there to look at the list."

I did not have anything to lose, so the three of us galloped down to the housemother's apartment to ask. I begged so pitifully she said I could go, as long as I came straight back.

Dashing up to the second floor, I passed Phillip coming down. He called out to me, "You got a part. I saw your name on the list." I ran even faster.

Yes, there was my name. I had been given the par)f the landlady. I would have been happy to get that part.. xcept at the top of the page Helen Hackett was listed as tl lead. That's just perfect, I thought to myself.

It was just a couple of weeks before finals when hillip asked me to meet him after lab. "I've got to talk to som ody," he said. He sounded really upset. "Helen is pregnant

I was stunned. "What are you going to do?"

"We're going to get married. We don't have any ioice. Helen's going to have to drop out of school."

I wish I could tell you I kept that information to yself. I didn't. I came straight back to the dorm and told Susai Then I went down the hall to Dottie's room. "Helen Ha ett is pregnant," I told her and her roommate. "Don't tell anybody."

I headed down to the shower room. There were six or seven girls getting ready for dinner. I said, "I sure was sad to hear about Helen Hackett."

"What about Helen?" they asked.

"She's leaving school," I replied. "She's pregnant, but whatever you do, don't tell anybody." They promised they wouldn't.

I cruised up to the third floor to ask Mary Ann about our psychology exam. "Isn't it a shame about Helen Hackett?" I said on my way out of her room. I did not stop until I had talked to every girl in our dormitory. Well, actually, I told every girl but June. She wasn't in her room. I had to come back later that night to take her into my confidence.

After telling June, I headed back to my room. I plopped down on my bed opposite Susan. I looked at her and said,

"Helen Hackett is pregnant." We began to laugh. We sat on our beds and held our sides and laughed because Helen Hackett was pregnant. She was going to have to leave school. Her life was ruined. Our laughter became more hysterical.

Susan looked at me. She said, "Helen couldn't."

"Couldn't what?" I asked.

"Hack it," she answered. We laughed again.

And then we began to cry. We fell into each other's arms and we wept because Helen Hackett was pregnant. Because Helen Hackett had to leave school. Because Helen Hackett had ruined her life. Because Helen was just perfect.

And if she couldn't hack it, our lives were so fragile, what chance did we have?

ELIZABETH: Working the emotional timeline was an important exercise for me. It put me in touch with emotions I had managed to bury. I had not thought of this incident in years. When I did think of it, I was always ashamed of my behavior.

The first issue for me was ownership. Could I publicly own what I had done? Was I willing for my listeners to know this about me? Was I willing to admit to such petty and revolting behavior? I really did not like the idea of having people know I was capable of doing something like this. It would have been very easy to go into denial about the whole thing. I spent some time journaling about my feelings. I realized my reluctance was based on unwillingness to take responsibility for what I had done. I came to feel that I could not urge others to stretch their comfort zone if I was not willing to do so as well.

Next, I needed to deal with issues of permission. I was willing to have people know about me. I did not, however, have the right to share the information about someone else without their permission. I thought about trying to contact the main character and rejected the idea. I decided it was too big an invasion of her privacy. Since we have not been in contact in nearly four decades, it was inappropriate of me to intrude into her life. This decision was, I admit, partly based on my unwillingness to tell her what I had done, even after all these years.

I decided instead to change enough of the facts to protect her privacy. So I changed her name and several of the details in the story. But I did not whitewash what I did. I left my own failure, my wickedness straightforwardly true to the facts.

I was sure everyone has had similar feelings of jealousy about someone. I chose the recurring phrase "just perfect" and wove it into the story. As I tell it, my listeners begin to chime in o those words. Sometimes, I don't even say them myself, I simply gesture to the listeners. They are happy to fill them in. I believe th helps them identify with my experience at a deeper level as th story unfolds.

· · ·

For the same conference workshop, Loren Niemi also used the emotional timeline to craft a personal-experience story n the theme of jealousy.

—————————————————————————————LOREN NIEMI—

Seeing Miss Julie

One warm spring morning, I left Omaha early and st, as was my habit. Just get in the car and drive to Minneapolis, I thought. I started off on the freeway, kicking cruise control up to 65 to 70—OK, 80 to 85—and watched the farm fields sail by. At some point I exited the freeway, made a turn onto a two-lane blacktop, and crossed a flat horizon stretching from one small town to another where silo, grain elevator, and church steeple are the only things rising above the land. Here and there stood little square white houses, monuments to hard work and simple living. In farm fields the tractors chugged along the fence lines to complete morning chores. The fields were all green promise. It was still early enough in the growing season not to know whether the cost of hope and a summer's toil would be profit or another farm auction.

About nine I stopped for coffee in one of those small towns along the way. There are two kinds of places to eat in those towns, the franchise that sits at the edge of town and the other place. The place the locals go. The place that looks a little run down, with the big table in the middle of the room surrounded by eight chairs where the local business guys or farmers in overalls drink coffee and talk crops, machinery, and everything except what they really feel.

Because I was a single man, I was seated where the single men are always seated—at a corner table. I looked at the menu but would order the usual stuff, two eggs over easy with hash browns, bacon on the side, toast, and a cup of coffee. Maybe some orange juice in a nod to healthy eating. I ordered. It arrived. I was enjoying the meal when I happened to glance over and see her sitting three tables away, by the window.

At first I just saw the gesture, a simple gesture seen from the corner of my eye. When I turned to look, really look, I had to look hard. It certainly looked like her. Miss Julie. I had always called her that. A woman I had gone out with many years before. A truly playful relationship marked by misadventure and letting go. She was just nineteen then, straight off a Red River Valley potato farm, looking for some big-city fun. It ended two years later when she said one day, I'm going skiing, and I knew that was it. She went to Colorado and from there to California. When I last heard from her, she was living in Huntington Beach.

So here's this older woman, blond, with the same kind of hair, done pretty much in the same kind of way. The same features, except she looked like Miss Julie should look twenty years later. Or at least how I thought she should look. The eyes a little sadder perhaps, the mouth wearing a smile harder fixed and not as quick to laughter as it had once been.

The waitress came over and poured me more coffee. I was still stuck on that gesture, thinking about how Miss Julie had moved her hand that way a thousand times and now here it was again, performed by this woman in this town, when I finally noticed who she was with. On one side of the table sat a man who was probably her husband, or maybe her brother, and a child. Probably her son, maybe her nephew. Next to her was an older woman, perhaps his mother, perhaps hers. It was a classic family scene, utterly domestic, all of them having a quiet Sunday after-church breakfast.

In that moment I was intensely jealous of him. I wanted to be him. I wanted to be with her once more. In that moment, I was willing to forsake everything I had to live in a white box house indistinguishable from a half-dozen box houses just like it in every direction in this town and the next. Willing to go shopping at the local store without enough choice to make a decent meal. Willing to forsake the good wines, or the latte, for years of bitter coffee you could see the bottom of the cup through. Willing to drive an hour, or three, to another, bigger town for culture. Willing to look at the farm fields with their squared corners and the season clock turning the weeks between planting and harvest. Willing to live a life marked by church and grocery and school, by wedding dances, Cub Scout meetings and funeral dinners.

I was ready to slip that life on as if it were a comfortable shirt just to be with her again. Just to make her smile. Give up this restlessness and rootless nomadic life I had known so long. To see it for the lonely life it was.

When the waitress left, I turned to get up and go over to the table, introduce myself and see if it really was her, but she was gone.

Having suddenly lost my taste for breakfast, I took my check in hand and went to pay my bill. At that moment she came out of the ladies' room and our eyes met. Me standing there with ready cash and she with a startled glance, color draining from her face, as if she had just seen the last thing she ever expected to see. Her mouth opened to say something, perhaps my name, then she caught herself, remained silent. A sense of something fleeting, perhaps longing, perhaps a kind of jealousy of her own, flickered over her face as my only acknowledgment.

And in that glance I realized that as much as I might want to be rooted, settled, and in her arms, she had looked at me and wanted the opposite, to be rootless and gone. I was a reminder of another life and a repudiation of all that was now. She had walked out the door, and I followed. If it were a movie I would have said something, but it wasn't. I said nothing, watched them get in a car. As I got in mine I realized this was just one of those moments, as they say, when we long to embrace the devil we do not know.

LOREN: This story is based on an actual experience I had in a small town diner. Whether the woman whose gesture I noticed was Miss Julie is unimportant. What matters is that it was enough to prompt me to think about her and to explore some emotional responses to the idea that it could be her.

The first choice I made in shaping this material was to use the wickedness-loss continuum (which will be examined in detail in chapter 8) and look at it as a story about jealousy as loss, specifically about choices that are made in a particular moment and the consequences of those choices. The second was to frame the jealousy as something which is not exclusive to one person but may be shared. In a sense, the story is told as a response to grief, focused on what has been lost and cannot be recovered. The third choice was to tell it as a confession, to acknowledge my own jealousy and hers.

With these choices in mind, I then framed the story within the poetic image of landscape and ordinary life, and made the most mundane of events (seeing someone you think you know in a restaurant) the catalyst for jealousy. The intent of the story is not to have anyone feel sorry for me but to create an opportunity for the listener to see my jealousy as a sorrowful circumstance they may also experience. By doing that, I invite the audience to enter the emotional heart of the story by virtue of the fact that any one of us can see ourselves in a similar situation.

Inside the structure of the story, I do several things to shape the sense of loss. I begin with a description of farm fields, a familiar landscape that foreshadows the possibility of loss. This narrative invitation to bring the audience into the story grounds it and provides a contrast between my moving through a landscape and the fixed lives the other characters experience.

The story progresses with a version of Joseph Campbell' "Journey of the Hero" model: an invitation, an exchange, a challenge, a "triumph," and a return. These are not worked out in literal sense the way they are in the classic folktale, but more loosely, as a kind of movement from image to image within the story.

The invitation is accomplished with a single image: my leaving early in the morning. It is voluntary but still leads me to the unexpected adventure.

What serves as the moment of exchange in this story? In the classic model, I would meet someone for whom I would do a good deed, or from whom I would receive advice, directions, or a magical object. Here the exchange is the interaction with the waitress by ordering the meal. The decision to stop is arbitrary but nevertheless provides me with the opportunity to go into the restaurant. This puts me in the right place at the right time. I give the waitress my order, she gives me time to look around the room.

In this model, there is also the element of challenge. It begins with the gesture, which leads to recognition, and beyond that, to assumptions about the reasons Miss Julie is there and, finally, what it could mean for me to be a part of her life again.

The triumph (as it were) is the moment when we meet at the cash register. I have allowed myself to think this is about me, about my understanding of the situation, but she has her own responses. When we meet, I get some significant nonverbal feedback from her. It may only be about her own recognition of the circumstances but it undercuts my assumptions and provides an insight for both myself and the listener.

What is the return? The return is as simple as getting back into the car, getting back on the road, though I am not necessarily recognized as a hero or as transformed by anyone but myself.

—Grief

Grief is a difficult emotion to consider because it is so personal. While we have many sources of grief in our lives, we do not necessarily have many ways to express it. We are often im[patient] with ourselves and with others. We watch the movers put [the] last of the furniture in the van, then lock the door of the ho[use] we have called home. We leave the hospital after the cancer surgery or drive away from the funeral, saying to ourselves, "Get over it. It's time to move on." We speak as if you could wear away a stone by telling it that the water will have its effect, without letting the water do its work with the passage of time.

If you were to do a timeline about grief, where would you begin? Think in the largest of terms. People grieve about lots of things—the death of loved ones, of course, but lots of other things as well.

The teen years are often heavy grieving years because this is when we first begin to realize we may not get the life we have day-dreamed about. It is a time for trying out for things you want and experiencing the reality of not getting them. It is a time for facing the limitations of your physical body. It is a time for watching childhood, with its play and friendships, slip away amid raging hormones and cultural pressures. Holden Caulfield is not the only one who sees himself surrounded by hypocrites.

For adults, grief usually means loss, and loss takes many forms. Elizabeth is a single grandmother who makes her living as a professional storyteller. She was delighted she could persuade anyone to finance a house for her under those circumstances. She thought she would be overjoyed by the accomplishment. Instead, she wept all the way home from the closing. If you have a thirty-year mortgage, that means you are not going back to the Appalachian Mountains to live. You are going to go on living in the city, where that house is. You aren't going back "home" to live.

If you are grieving for the end of a marriage, others can relate to that. A job, a dream, a person, an event—no matter what you have grieved for, there are others for whom it will resonate. It doesn't make any difference how ordinary or simple it may seem to you, there are other people who are waiting to hear your experience. By giving voice to your experience, you create a way for them to voice theirs.

Grief

Time of Life	What happened	Effect
EARLY CHILDHOOD		
LATER CHILDHOOD		
TEEN		
YOUNG ADULT		
ADULT		
WHATEVER'S NEXT		

Once again, we can use the same basic form to chart our images of grief. And also once again, to represent the process of identifying grief, we look for the concrete images, the sensory expressions, of our sense of loss. The following story rises from a specific sensory image and puts us firmly in the seat of grief.

—MEGAN WELLS—
Thom's Dream

We weren't particularly close in college, Thom Miller and I. We worked as graduate assistants for the University Theatre box office. Our desks were right next to each other; our social lives, worlds apart. I was looking for love in all the wrong places. Thom was Snow White at the well, singing, *"Someday my prince will come..."* Our acquaintanceship revolved around food; we shared a mutual weakness for cheesecake, Eli's chocolate chip.

We graduated and moved to Chicago, M.F.A.s in hand, to launch our theater ambitions on the sea of the city, opening yet another off-off-Loop theater company. We managed crisis to crisis, show to show, for three years. Finally, we ran out of money, energy, and hope. Thom moved to Seattle to try his luck there. I found a corporate job. We promised to write. You know how it goes...

I thought about Thom every time I went to the theater, which wasn't often—it hurt too much to get too close to my lost dream. One night, I was seeing a play at Victory Gardens Theater. Before the second act I stopped for a gulp of water, annoyed by the skinny guy hogging the fountain. He turned.

"Thom Miller? What are you doing here?" We laughed right into hug. That's how I knew before he told me. I could feel his ribs through his shirt.

We skipped the second act. Over coffee and chocolate-chip cheesecake, we told each other our stories. He done fairly well in Seattle, but his debt finally brought him down. He'd accepted a job at Barat College in Lake Forest working the theater box office. "I meant to call you so many times." "Yeah, me too." Then, walking out the door of the coffee shop: "Megan?" "Yeah, Thom?" "I've got..." "I know."

While I drove him home, he told me how his prince had come at last, handsome, yes, but dark and with a past. Outside Thom's apartment he lingered in the car, his hand on the door handle. "You wouldn't happen to know anybody with a room to rent, would you?"

I'd been thinking about getting a roommate. I'd lucked into a huge two-bedroom in Wrigleyville but needed a break in the rent. "Why?" I asked.

"Well, my lease is up and... I was going to stay with a

friend for a couple of weeks, just until I could find a place..."
I waited. "She backed out..." I could hear his feet shuffling
on the floor mats. "She's afraid she'll catch it."

One week later Thom moved in with me. My boyfriend
worried. But Thom was careful to protect me, bleaching the
tub and basin every morning after his shower and shave.

The bathroom... seems like it all happened in the bathroom.
It was a Wednesday morning, 7:45 am. I was getting ready
for work. Thom's alarm went off. I wondered how he had
slept. We'd had a particularly tough weekend; his cough was
keeping him up at night—keeping us both up.

He came in. He was wearing his lime green p.j. bottoms,
thin cotton with a drawstring waist, his hair unruly—you
know what wonderful sculptures pillows can make. He put
down the toilet seat, sat, and said, "I had a dream..." I
watched him through the mirror. He leaned his elbows on his
knees to continue.

"I was on the beach, an ocean beach. My sister and her
husband and... yes, the kids were with us too. We were all
standing on an embankment, overlooking the ocean. Then
I saw other people, in the water... playing in the waves. And
then I was in the water. They were... tremendous... the waves.
Not violent, but powerful. They were..." He closed his eyes
for a moment, searching for a word. I held my breath.
"...tremendous.

"Suddenly, the sands shifted and I lost my balance. I was
being buffeted about. I started scrambling in the water, fighting to get my balance, but the more I fought, the more I
seemed to lose control.

"And then someone—I didn't know who, just a someone—
appeared and said, 'Lean into it... the wave... just lean into

the wave.' So I did. And then I was flying. It was... I kept leaning, and each time I leaned farther and farther till I was almost... flying." He gestured—his arms spread wide.

"Then there was this huge wave. Grand... bigger than anything... and it wrapped me up and I was pinned on the beach, up against the embankment. My arms pinned against the rocks and the wave just holding me, pressing me, pressing my chest so that I couldn't breath. It didn't hurt, no, but it frightened me. Really, really frightened me. I felt helpless, scared... alone. I remember knowing my sister was there but she couldn't help, she wasn't meant to help. I started to panic. Then I remembered...

"...I leaned."

He fell silent. I watched his eyes moving slowly back and forth behind closed lids. He straightened his upper body, a deep breath pressing the outline of his ribs against pink white flesh. He sighed, "It's hollow, but not empty, no... it's full... peaceful. I'm just hanging here, floating, leaning, and all around me is..." He started to cry. I watched, mesmerized, as a tear curled slowly, gently, over his long blonde lash and stopped. Hanging on his lash as he hangs in his wave. A crystal ball reflecting all the light we felt at that moment.

Then it was over, just that quick. He stood up, ran his fingers through his sandy hair, and started to go. At the door: "I guess it was more a vision than a dream, don't you think?"

He looked at me with such openness, I fell in. "Y . Yes, Thom, I think it was more of a vision than a dream. I told him he should write it down. "Oh, no need, I'll always remember," and he left the bathroom. His bare feet going my heartbeat on the floorboards.

After that dream, Thom and I practiced "leanin into"

everything. We spent hours with crayons and poster paper creating pictures of our dreams and fears. We gorged on books about mysticism and soul and death and love. We went to all the movies and always got popcorn. I pulled out my theater dream, polished it up along with my resume, and launched my hopes again.

Two months later, Thom made a decision. He moved back to Seattle and regathered his group of artist friends. They put together a production of Samuel Beckett's *Endgame*, then toured the production around the West Coast. At the end of a year, when Thom was too weak to tour, he moved in with his sister, her husband, and children, who live in a big house on an embankment overlooking the ocean. I often imagined him at night, lying in bed, listening to the waves.

Toward the end, when he was in the hospital, Thom wouldn't let me come see him. He said he needed me to remember him as he was. One night, when we were on the phone, he was in terrible pain and I tried to soothe him. "Thom, Thom, remember your dream? Your vision of the waves?"

"No, Megan, what vision?"

I couldn't sleep that night. I wrote down everything I could remember about our morning in the bathroom and mailed it to him.

When he got it, he called me: "Megan? I'm leaning now." A few days later, Thom Miller died.

We're back to being acquaintances again. I go whole months sometimes without remembering him. But when I'm questioning my life, when the waves of fear threaten to overwhelm me, when I'm running low on money or energy or hope, I remember Thom's dream . . . and I lean.

MEGAN: This story is the first one I ever wrote, and it lau ched me into the world of storytelling. It began just as th story says—sending a few lines about Thom's dream to him w ːn he had forgotten and most needed to remember. After Thoː died, I was so stirred up by the realization that people carry drea s and stories for each other that I felt it was morally necessary ɪr me to tell Thom's story in some fashion.

The work of writing was both easy and difficult. Sinc t was a real event, I had the plot and events already. The difficuˌty was shaping the story. What should I keep? What is too much? What is too little? I focused on the details and edited out my own feelings wherever I could. In that way, the listeners get to have their feelings and I'm out of the way.

For years, this story was hidden inside a much larger frame about my relationship with my mother. After telling it over and over, I realized that it was weighed down by the framework. So I stripped away everything that wasn't necessary to explain the dream and then the story came fully alive.

I wrestled with this story for three years before I actually told it, because I could not give myself permission to speak about AIDS. I felt as if I were borrowing from a tragedy that I did not fully understand, and I did not want to insult anyone with the disease. Then I realized that the story wasn't really about AIDS, at least not directly. It isn't the "what" Thom was dying of, it is about "how" Thom lives with his dying.

This story is my grieving for Thom. It both celebrates him and lets him go. Each time I tell it, I feel the simplicity and power of his dream and feel grateful. And always when I tell it, someone will come up after and share a story of his own.

MEGAN WELLS *is a storyteller, corporate and community storytelling consultant, writer, and theater artist who resides on the outskirts of Chicago.*

· · ·

No matter what emotion you name, you can do the timeline exercise and come up with potential material. The key to the timeline is to give yourself permission to name the emotion as a sense image—not the idea, but the experience. What did this powerful emotion look like, sound like, taste like, smell like, feel like? Think about the representation of longing and loss in Orson Welles's *Citizen Kane* that is attached to "Rosebud," the image of a child's sled.

Whatever material you decide to shape from this, it may not be something you can tell tomorrow. As Megan points out, it may take months or years of living with this material before you are ready to tell it. The apple tree does not begin with fruit ripe, ready to be picked, but with blossoms awaiting pollination. Though it may be a long way to the public utterance, that does not mean that you should not identify the emotional issues that matter to you and begin to call the stories forth.

The use of the emotional timeline discussed in this chapter can help you identify many experiences in your life that are the seeds of stories. Here are some suggestions of emotions for which constructing a timeline might prove useful.

Jealousy   Grief   Anger   Fear   Revenge

Embarrassment   Wonder   Frustration   Desire

Joy   Pride   Passion   Hope   Reverence

Select an emotion you want to explore. Anger and desire are close to the surface and usually quite easy to access. Grief and happiness, both of which we are taught to deny, may be buried in deeper emotional recesses. Initially, we would suggest that you pick any emotion that you readily respond to. Later, after you've had some practice with this exercise, you may want to select emotions that you have a harder time accessing or are particularly troubled by.

Across the top of a page make three column headings, and down the left side, list the stages of your life, like this:

Time of Life	What happened	Effect
EARLY CHILDHOOD		
LATER CHILDHOOD		
TEEN		
YOUNG ADULT		
ADULT		

For Adulthood use (roughly) ten-year intervals.

continued on next page

Fill in the first category with moments and sensations. As much as possible, do not fill in plot elements but sense images and metaphors.

- How did something look, smell, taste?

- What did it sound like?

- What would symbolize the moment and your experience of the emotion in the moment?

Let your memory and imagination float across the surface of this personal historical landscape. There is no right answer. There is no need to try to force an image.

After you have filled in the "What Happened" column, fill in the next one. In some instances the effect will be clear and immediate. In others there may be no obvious result. Again, do not force yourself to put anything on paper. If there is something there, take a look at it and ask yourself:

- How or why did the one lead to the other?

- Is there a pattern of cause and effect that repeats itself in your life?

- What other emotions are called to mind or connected with this one?

- Which of the images you have identified is the seed of a story?

- What kind of a story is it?

- What will you have to do to be able to tell it?

SEVEN

Structural Elements Used in the Creation of Stories

The true art of memory is the art of attention.
—Dr. Samuel Johnson

There is something of a "chicken or the egg" problem in the shaping of the difficult story. You can decide on the structural elements first and build the story afterwards. You can also begin to shape the raw material and make the decisions about which structural elements should be used to give the story the proper weight and form once you know what the story is. We have done both.

In this and the following chapters we will begin with the assumption that you are choosing to work with the structural elements first and shaping the material accordingly. The structural elements or choices about how to tell the story we will examine are:

- tone (comic or tragic)
- point of view
- point of entry
- wickedness-loss continuum
- emotional arc
- moral framework

—Tone

What's funny about breast cancer? Why would anyone want to laugh about the loss of life? Or about a moral failing that religious folks would call sin?

The first decision—is it comedy or tragedy—is a critical one. It is our belief that any story can be told as comedy or tragedy. One is not necessarily better than the other. Both can serve the needs of the teller and the listener. It is not the subject matter that dictates the appropriate choice but your purpose in telling the story. It is a matter of individual style and specific choice. What effect you want to achieve may suggest one approach is preferable to another. Skillful tellers can often find a way to incorporate both within the same story.

The value of telling a story as comedy comes from the recognition that laughter is the great leveler, the solvent of human emotion. When we laugh, tension is released. We can see how our assumptions have been misplaced. For all of our pretense to dignity, our feet remain firmly planted on the banana peel.

Suppose you were suffering from an inoperable brain tumor and slipping toward death by degrees. This is clearly a difficult story to tell. Would you choose to focus on the loss of opportunity that your illness represented or to seize on the joyous moments that remain? Before her death, storyteller Katie Rubio chose to laugh about the absurdities of hospitalization and the innumerable medical procedures to which she was subjected. In choosing to laugh, she celebrated her living and helped dispel the fear we often face when dealing with a life-threatening illness.

Spalding Gray tells thought-provoking stories from his life that are quite funny. One of his best-known stories, "Sex and Death to Age Fourteen," is basically about dead pets and masturbation. It is a perfect example of presenting material many people would never think of sharing. The material piques our curiosity, and by saying that which is potentially embarrassing to himself, he helps us remember our own experiences at a similar age.

Any subject can be presented as comedy or tragedy. Steven Spielberg gave us one version of the Holocaust as *Schindler's List*. Roberto Benini presented us another in *Life Is Beautiful*. Each of them has presented a very different kind of picture of the same event. Each of them has made high art from that tragic experience; a thoroughly moral art from what was for many people the end of the world.

In choosing the tragic, one gives voice to core emotions. In the tragic we might find the cleansing of tears and the fulsome gravitation of human limits. From Sophocles to Shakespeare to Charles Dickens to Maya Angelou, the rise and fall of humanity has been told with much compassion and clarity in tragedy.

The difficulty with choosing the tragic voice is that we must be masters of the emotional tone and not its servant. When the teller is overwhelmed by the tragedy of a story, he loses the clarity that lets the listener respond to the material. The focus shifts from the story to the teller of the tale. The most common way this happens is when the teller fails to structure the story so as to allow himself to remain outside the emotion it contains. Tellers cry. They rage. They attack the listener for complacency or failure to understand. Swept away by their emotions, they get lost or confused. The story suffers as a result; rather than invite the listener in, it holds them at a distance.

There are times when a story is so powerful that it is not possible to get, or stay, outside the material. Elizabeth's "Demeter and Persephone, 1984" is an example. Loren has witnessed Holocaust survivors who in telling their lives have reached a point where they are unable to speak another word. Their silence is testimony to the scale of the tragedy. We are not suggesting that in such circumstances one should choose comedy. We are suggesting when one chooses to tell a story that is overwhelmingly tragic, part of owning it is preparing yourself and your listeners for what will follow.

There is no hard and fast rule about how to determine if a story should be humorous or serious. Even in the tragic, introducing humor can be beneficial. A good laugh can break the tension. It can keep a topic from getting too morose.

Comic relief can be as helpful to the teller as to the listener. Telling some difficult stories is like driving an eighteen-wheeler. Sometimes the weight you are pulling and the speed with which you are moving can become overwhelming. You can feel the load beginning to shift. It's getting away from you. It's going to jack-knife, and the wreck is going to be painful. Interjecting humor at that point can help you regain your balance. It can help you get your wheels back on the pavement. Building humor in from the start is a good way to prevent becoming engulfed by the emotion of the story.

This is often an issue of comfort. What is the teller's relationship to his or her listeners? How much common ground do teller and listener share? An AIDS sufferer might tell his story as pratfall, satire, or knowing stand-up comedy to other AIDS sufferers because they share common ground. This does not mean that the AIDS sufferer might not use laughter to tell his story to a non-suffering audience, but it is not the same. The laughter that rises from shared experience is much freer than what is understood by those who have not tasted bitter fruit. Richard Pryor's or Chris Rock's scathing comedy about the African–American experience means something quite different to white audiences than to black ones. One audience visits a different place, the other lives there.

One should not assume that a serious story is the best way to tackle a serious subject. One should not assume that comedy will protect a teller or an audience from the pain of a serious subject. One should not assume, period. One should look at the specifics of the teller, the tale, and the listener. What is the capacity of the one telling the story to make his meaning clear? Is he telling the story or is the story telling him? Can he tell the difficult story in a way that invites the audience to enter it fully? What approach best serves the story, the teller, and the listener? This is always the first question that must be answered in determining whether to choose comedy, tragedy, or some combination of the two.

—Point of View

Let us turn our attention to which point of view the story will be told from. Stories are usually told in the first or third person. Occasionally the second-person point of view may be employed. That's it: *I, he/she,* and *you.* This is the full range of choices for point of view. Each can liberate or imprison us within the story.

When you tell a story in the first person, in the voice of *I,* several things happen. First, you cannot tell anything more in the story than the narrator would actually know. So if we are telling the story of a tornado or a murder, we cannot know what other characters in the story know or feel unless they convey that information to us in some direct way. Everything about the action and characters in the story passes through the filter of the first-person narrator's observation, assumptions, thought, and judgment.

In the first-person story, there is only one point of view. The teller must own it. When the story is narrated by a character within the story, the teller must give himself permission to truly speak from that character's view of the world. This may mean speaking discomforting words—if the first-person narrator is a racist, as an example. The listener must be able to understand what is happening based solely on what the narrator says and her "tone" of voice.

When you tell in the third person, there is permission to be omniscient by virtue of the fact you are outside the story. You can speak for and about everyone in the tale. You may jump around in time. You may view the action from different perspectives. You may tell what everyone thinks, feels, knows, and does. It is both a blessing and a curse. The blessing is, all things are possible. The curse is, it still has to make sense.

One of the benefits of this choice is that the audience gets to take a step back from you as the storyteller. They don't necessarily need to identify the story with you personally. In telling certain kinds of difficult stories, this may be of great value.

In some circumstances, Loren tells the story of the death of his daughter, Hannah. It is a story that focuses on what constitutes happiness and what happens when it is torn away. He always tells it in the third person. He tells it in the third person of necessity, because it retains a powerful emotional hold on him and telling it in the first person is always an invitation to tears. He tells it in the third person by choice, because it allows the audience to think about what the death of a child means for a father without getting caught up in thinking that Loren is the father in question.

He was asked to tell it once at the Illinois Storytelling Festival. His natural inclination to being careful in the sorrow of the telling was doubled by the fact that it was the eleventh anniversary of Hannah's death. Afterwards, a woman who did not know this was his personal story came up to him and told him that while she liked the story, she would have liked it better if the child had lived. He agreed that he also would have liked it better if the child had lived, but since this was a true story, he couldn't change the ending.

Would the woman have said anything to him if he had told it in the first person? She might have offered condolences, but she certainly would not have heard the story the same way. It is unlikely that she would have considered how she wanted the story to end, if it was told as a personal tragedy rather than as a universal one. Here is that story:

—LOREN NIEMI—
Hannah on a Summer's Day

July 24th. It is one of those summer afternoons that redeems Minnesota, making you forget winter as the sun pours molten gold through the leafy canopy.

In the backyard, a classic scene: the grill fired up, a steady column of white smoke from the charcoal, laced with wet applewood, rises from the vent. A man sits tending the grill. Periodically he removes the black dome to prod or poke at the coals, but mostly he sits watching the shadows as they creep from the flower beds in search of night. Mostly he sits holding his baby daughter, Hannah, and tells her, though he knows she does not understand, about grilling trout and sweet corn.

About how just this morning her mother bought the corn from a red-haired little girl sitting on the tailgate of a pickup, with a green mountain of freshly picked ears beside her. How the leaves of corn were carefully pulled back, the silk removed, and the rows of captured sunlight were rubbed with butter and wrapped with fresh mint before the leaves were put back in place. He rocks the baby in his arm as he tells her how the corn was laid on the fire to roast in its own leaves. Though she has no teeth, he tells her of the pleasure to be found in pulling off the blacked leaves of roasted corn and biting into the hot sweetness of corn cooked in butter, mint, and its own juices.

Then he tells her how he had stopped at the fish shop on the way home and selected two quicksilver trout, each a little more than a pound with heads and tails intact. He tells her about washing the trout with cold water, then stuffing the cavity which had contained their life with pieces of pear, mushroom, sage, and ripe black olives. How he rubbed their skins with a thin coating of olive oil. When the corn is nearly done he will lay the fish on the fire, five minutes to a side.

"You'll probably be asleep when this happens," he says, "but because you are my only daughter, I want to tell you what makes me happy."

He sits back in the chair and looks at his Hannah, and sees that she is the very reason he could even say such a thing. He had never imagined happiness for himself, had never spoken the words "I am happy" because he had never believed it, never felt an emotion that he could identify as sure, unqualified happiness. Even when he was in love, when he was with her mother, he had been reluctant to say that he was happy. This had created some difficulties, but his wife had come to understand that like many men of his generation, he was suspect of emotions in general and of happiness in particular.

Hannah looks at him, her eyes not quite yet focused, and smiles the incandescent smile that babies have. It is blissful, a half-awake, half-asleep smile, and always, it seems, on the edge of dreaming. Now he holds her up, her round face like a serene Buddha. She waves her balled fists as if beating the clouds. He stands and lifts her again, so that she might feel the warmth of the sun. She makes a gurgling sound and he looks at her against the blue sky, straining to see if she is upset. She is not. It is just a baby sound but he sits down again, cradling her in his arms and wondering how he came to be so blessed.

They sit like this for a long time. He thinks about being a father, about his own father, and wonders if his father ever felt this way about him. He thinks that his father would have, must have, did, but they do not talk much and have never talked about happiness, or even about being a father. He thinks about his friends, the ones who used to drink in bars and chase women, the ones that used to play softball and throw a hastily packed suitcase into the back of a car to drive two-lane blacktop highways in search of bad food and misadventure.

Things changed when they got married. You might not see them as often, but you still got together. But when they became fathers, well, when they became fathers there was still that brag and bluster, and new complaints or jokes about diapers. Yet something was different. You could see it in their eyes, in the way they held themselves, but no one spoke of it. They did not talk about the reality of fatherhood, the realization that you would change, would want to change, would admit that you were under the spell of a helpless, eating, shitting, soft-fleshed wonder you called your child.

It was overwhelming. So much so that some ran away, unable to face their responsibility. Even in their departure they were marked. He didn't know if it was fear or understanding that drove them away, but in this late afternoon of a summer's day with Hannah, he understood that he could not leave, would never want to leave her. Why let go of this happiness he could not speak and perhaps should not say aloud? He had no words to explain it and no desire to impoverish these feelings with description. So he stopped thinking about how to articulate his joy and simply sat inside this perfect moment.

Mostly the baby slept. Her mouth open, a thin trail of drool running along her cheek. He laughed to himself at the thought her mother did this when she slept as well.

His wife came out of the house and sat with him. She asked if he wanted her to hold the baby while he cooked, but he was reluctant to give up this feeling of contentment. He turned the corn as he held Hannah in his arms. He and the wife sipped a glass of pale champagne, the bubbles rising like golden balls before the departing sun's warmth. When everything was ready, they took the fish, the corn, the champagne, the baby, and went into the house. The baby went into the crib, the rest on the table with slices of buttered warm bread to make it a perfect meal.

After supper, he went in to look at Hannah. He could not stop himself from picking her up, carrying her to their bedroom and lying down with her, still sleeping on his chest. He could feel her milky breath on his skin and feel her warmth. Once again that sensation came over him, that feeling that this was what it meant to be happy, and the tears ran down his cheeks. He did not want the moment to end. He could not imagine asking for anything more.

This is how the story ends: she died that night. And when she died, he knew that he could never bear being happy again.

Other times you may want to have the listeners acknowledge that the person in the story and the person telling the story have some kind of shared identity. When we tell from a voice of confession or guilt, the first-person narration often gives moral weight to the story. (Think of the voice of the narrator in Edgar Allan Poe's "The Tell-Tale Heart.")

Suppose we are telling a traditional tale; for this example, we will use "Mister Fox." Generally "Mister Fox" is told in the third person, as it was in Elizabeth's example. It is about the actions of Polly and those of Mister Fox. What is said is put in an "objective" or neutral voice. The plot elements are told without necessarily favoring one or the other character's point of view. We know what Polly does. We know what Mister Fox does. In most versions of the story, we don't know why they do what they do or how they feel about it. In folktales, generally the action is described but not the internal thought or feelings of the characters. The teller could assign motivation to them, but generally does not.

Suppose we were to tell "Mister Fox" from the first person point of view. We would have to decide whether to tell it from the point of view of Polly, or that of Mister Fox. To choo Mister Fox's point of view presents some problems. Listener could be very unsympathetic. We would be telling from the p nt of view of "Bluebeard" or a serial killer. It would be difficult t make the listeners suspend judgment long enough to listen o his truth. Their basic impulse is to hate Mister Fox.

Not only is there the unsympathetic audience to c tend with, there is also the fact that in the traditional version, Mister Fox dies at the end. It is pretty hard to speak in the first person when dead! (It can be done, though. Ambrose Bierce's "An Occurrence at Owl Creek Bridge" and the movie *American Beauty* are both narrated from that point of view.)

In telling the story from the third person you do not have the same problem. In the traditional story, Polly triumphs, and it is told from outside her consciousness.

One of the great blessings in utilizing third-person narrative is you can describe landscape and insert culture or history into the story much more easily than in first-person narrative. In Elizabeth's traditional version of "Mister Fox," the setting of the story is organic to the cultural framework; this would be much more difficult to achieve in the first person.

The second person is the most difficult point of view. In this narrative approach, the listeners are addressed directly as if they are the protagonist in the story. The success of this narration rests entirely on whether or not the listener is willing to assume that they understand who the "you" in the story is. It can work and work well, but to do so it must be crafted with great clarity.

Consider, for example, this passage: "You thought you were so smart, didn't you? Just rush through the job and get it done. Take the easy way out and then play. Your brother did the same thing and look where it got him. The both of you. Living in run-down houses. Straw? What kind of building material is that? Sticks? Like we were in some third-world slum . . . The first time the wolf is at the door, it's run for my house." It is pretty easy in this instance to make the leap to "The Three Little Pigs."

Most listeners have enough information to be able to match what they are hearing to a story they know well. But what if the listener is a Hmong or Ethiopian immigrant who has not grown up in a culture where they would hear this folktale? How would they understand who the "you" might be?

The task in the second-person narrative is to help the listener piece together the "you" in a way that does not insult them or diminish the story. It requires a kind of careful elegance to find the balance between how the "you" is addressed and the amount of information that must be shared with the audience to keep them interested.

—Point of Entry

The example of "The Three Little Pigs" can also serve as an introduction for the discussion of point of entry. Where you begin the story may be as important as who is telling it. In that example, the use of the second person "you" allows for a point of entry that is not the traditional beginning but further along the chronological plotline. This point of entry allows us to do two things: characterize the narrator by what and how he speaks; and condense the early elements of the plot in favor of a more detailed development of the third segment or the relationships of the three pigs to each other.

While every story has a beginning, middle, and end, the place to start is not necessarily at the chronological beginning. Sometimes it keeps us from getting to the real core or meaning of the story. Sometimes it is not clear where the point of entry actually is or should be. It may be at the point where the world is turned upside-down. It may be at the point where the extraordinary intersects the everyday. Sometimes you enter the house proudly through the front door. Sometimes you sneak into the house, as the blues guys put it, as "a back door man." Sometimes you don't enter the house at all but can get a pretty good understanding of what's going on by merely looking in the window.

The point of entry is a space, a doorway, which allows you and the listener to find common ground. The point of entry may take many forms but always serves as an invitation for the listener to come into the story with the teller.

In the telling of difficult stories, the selection of the point of entry is worth careful consideration, both because it serves as the portal into the story and because it is usually closely linked to the narrator's point of view. In a first-person narrative, the point of entry frames how the listener hears the tale. In a third-person narration, the point of entry often presents the style and rhythm of the story.

In Loren's story "Mitterand's Last Meal," the point of entry is actually a sly reversal of the dialogue between the heroine and the wolf in "Little Red Riding Hood." It sets the psychological tone for the story and serves as a commentary. It also models the two distinct threads that are woven through the tale: the desire to have, to consume, what is forbidden and the power of ambiguous or ironic association of one thing with another to make the whole more than the sum of its parts.

In the traditional folk or fairy tale, the point of entry is usually a formula: *"Once upon a time..."* In those few code words, the listener is asked to put aside logic, suspend disbelief, and accept what follows as metaphoric rather than factual. Folk and fairy tales also usually end with formulas of reassurance and closure, *"happily ever after"* being the most common in our culture.

When telling a difficult story, there is also a need for reassurance or closure. Like the traditional story beginning or ending, it serves to frame the material and allow the listeners passage out of the timeless or metaphoric and back into their everyday world. What is an appropriate form of closure? All we can suggest is that it must support both the meaning of the story and the relationship of the teller to the listener. The use of a moral lesson, as an example, may be appropriate for a church setting but would be seen as coy—or worse, insulting—by an audience used to the ambiguities of performance art.

Both the point of entry and the ending of a story should convey a sense of completeness. As listeners, we want to be invited into the story right away, not left standing around waiting. Once inside, however, we don't want to leave until we are ready. Like leaving after a good meal, we want to be full but don't want to stay around to clean the dishes. When it's time to go, there should be a sense of having seen and heard enough.

Tone

Select a traditional story you know well or one from your life. Do some journaling around the following questions: How can it be told as a comedy? How can it be told as tragedy? How many of the elements are the same? Where do you place the emphasis in each version? If it is a comedy, does it move toward a single punchline or does it feature multiple opportunities for laughter? Is the laughter based on overstatement, exaggeration, and excess, or understatement and irony?

Who is the hero in each version? What is the task? What are the challenges? The lessons to be learned? The gifts and shadows to be acknowledged within the story?

Point of View

Select a traditional story that you know well or one from your own life. Think about telling it in the first person, then about telling it in the third person. Make two columns on a sheet of paper. Mark one "first person" and the other "third person." Note the answers to the following questions:

- Where is the narrator located in the story?

- Is the story told in the present or the past tense?

- What does the narrator know? How is that revealed to the listener?

- How does the narrator feel about his or her circumstances, decisions, actions, and relationships with other characters in the story?

Write one version of the story from the first or third person point of view.

continued on next page

The next day, write it again, using another character who is in the story—again from a first or third person point of view.

Compare the two. If it looks like the same story, you haven't gotten out of your point of view. Try it again. Each character should tell, substantially, a different kind of story based on their role and point of view.

Point of Entry

Select a traditional story that you know well or one from your own life. On a piece of paper or in a journal write out the progression of the story. What is the beginning? What follows that? What is the end?

Now make another progression, this time starting from the middle of the same story. If you begin here, how is the listener introduced to the situation? What information do you have to provide the listener at the beginning and what can you introduce as you go along to arrive at the same ending? Throw away whatever you think you have to provide at the beginning. What happens if you substitute detail and action for explanation?

Now make a third progression, this time starting with the end. Look at the first progression you have written and ask yourself how else you could have arrived here. What other path will take you to the same destination?

Bonus Exercise

What would happen if you began at the end and worked backwards to the so-called beginning? How would you make the regression in time, the links between one event and what preceded it, clear? How would you make it interesting? Is the beginning a natural place to arrive from this conclusion?

A Wickedness-Loss
Continuum

The rose is gone from the Garden;
what shall we do with the thorns?
— Sufi master, Hakim Jami

Some of us want to avoid the shadow side of our experience,
focusing only on the positive. Yet seldom do we arrive at our destination by the straight path or a simple decision. We have to laugh
at the absurdity of being human. We have to admit that there are
times when pride and stupidity keep us from being the saints we
would like to be. As we observed earlier, we all have some of Jung's
Trickster within us: our head in the clouds, our feet in the mud,
with everything in between concerned with sex and the belly. The
very act of telling where and how we fail or embrace the shadow
is life-affirming. It reminds our listeners of our shared humanity. Hence the necessity for acknowledging wickedness and loss.

To fully tell the truth we must say that we have experienced
so-and-so, that we felt such-and-such. It is not always clear how
it happened. It is not always clear what it means. There are times
when we are not sure how we feel about what happened. The decision to tell the difficult story is not always about surety, but often
about choice. We decide. We act. We tell. We shape the telling.

In the process, what we are not clear about may come into focus.

In thinking about the topic of this book, we believe that all difficult stories are in one way or another about wickedness and loss. We can see in every story how varying degrees of choice and circumstance, gift and shadow, inform our understanding of what happened and what it means.

—The Continuum as Story Tree

For our purposes, you might metaphorically think of wickedness and loss as a continuum or as a tree, with an event in our life as the roots or trunk and *Wickedness* and *Loss* as the first branches. For each of those polarities there are four additional branches that are ways of responding to the event, and for each of the responses there are four "twigs" (voices) that we can use to help us further shape the story. On these twigs will hang the necessary point of view, details, and descriptions that are the "fruit" of the story that we will share with an audience.

Possible difficult story topics:
violence – abuse – rape – betrayal – revenge – divorce
alcoholism – drug addiction – masturbation – incest – adultery
homosexuality – jealousy – despair – suicide – illness – death
natural disaster – accident – disability – racism – prejudice
pride – gluttony – sloth – theft – anger – lust – envy

For any topic there are two fundamental polarities:

Wickedness	Loss
(WHAT IS CHOSEN)	(WHAT IS IMPOSED)

What do we mean when we use the word *wicked?* How do we own our wickedness? What do we mean when we use the word *loss?* How do we accept our loss? It is helpful to understand what we mean by wickedness and loss, for the meanings

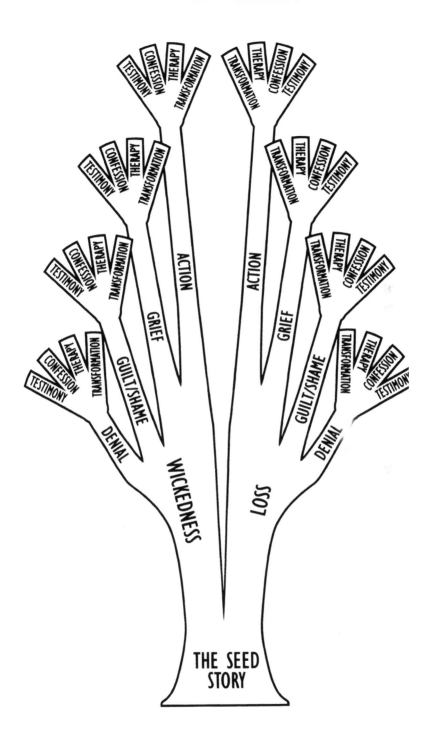

of both are rich in nuance and emotion.

We need to see that these words *wickedness* and *loss,* which we use to characterize internal and external circumstance, as well as the world itself, are multidimensional. We want to acknowledge complexity, the fact of joy and sorrow, hope and despair, as intertwined realities. We want to be willing to metaphorically stand naked in the process of telling our lives. We want to show the world the curve of tired flesh, the scars, the lines on our face that experience has given us.

When we talk about the stories of wickedness, we refer to stories about what has been chosen. What I choose. What we chose. Or what another has chosen. They are about what is conscious. They are about failure and about what happens when one makes bad choices. They are about what, in religious terms, might be called evil or sin, the imposition of our will on the world. *Wickedness,* for our purposes, refers to those things that are internal, those things that we have some degree of control over or complicity in, what we have done or failed to do.

At the other polarity are stories of loss, which are the stories of circumstance. *Loss* represents the intersection of other realities on ours. It is what comes from outside and is not chosen but imposed upon us. Loss may be seen as a trial, or as is often portrayed in religious terms, a test, which we must suffer through or learn to accept. Loss almost always begins with that which is outside our choices. When we talk of loss we usually mean things like disease, accident, and the unexpected.

Let us move on to the next segment, the metaphoric branches of the story tree.

For any topic there is a continuum of response:

Denial	Guilt/Shame	Grief	Action
(MY REJECTION)	(MY FAILURE)	(MY LOSS)	(MY CHOICE)

The first possible response to any difficult story topic, whether it is grounded in wickedness or loss, is *denial*. Denial is a kind of lie we tell ourselves. *This is not what happened. This is not what my experience really was.* We do not want to admit the facts. In denial our pain is so great we offer ourselves some other explanation other than our choice or the circumstance we find ourselves in for what happened.

The second possible response is *guilt*. Here we have a sense of ourselves as participating in what happened. Guilt may be seen in terms of responsibility or a judgment of failure that we place on ourselves. It may also be expressed as blame: we blame ourselves, or others blame us.

The third response is *grief*, wherein we recognize that something was lost. We know that something has changed that cannot be recovered or restored. The most common response to this is emotional pain or a deep sense of regret for that which might have been. We weep to release our pain.

Finally we have the response of *action*, in which we take responsibility for what happened. Here we actively engage the situation and do something about the challenge at hand. It is in the active response that we can model those behaviors that solve or resolve difficulties. This does not necessarily mean "for the better." In some instances the resolution to a difficulty is not for the better, but it may be sufficient to get us unstuck.

For any response there can be a continuum of "voice":

Testimony   Confession   Therapy   Transformation

$\begin{pmatrix}\text{WHAT}\\\text{HAPPENED}\end{pmatrix}$ (RESPONSIBILITY) (UNDERSTANDING) $\begin{pmatrix}\text{MODELING}\\\text{CHANGE}\end{pmatrix}$

We understand that the way we have organized the chart is, by its very nature, an arbitrary device. We do not necessarily need to use these categories and could just as easily have chosen others that could provide a filter for shaping our stories. They present us with a range of emotional and moral responses. They are a way of sorting through our "how do we feel about this" landscape and the different tones of voice available to us to use in telling the difficult story.

This process may seem unnecessarily complicated. Be patient. We are trying to find a way of talking about how to work with material that is often emotionally difficult or overlaid with religious and moral considerations without oversimplifying it or making it more complicated than it actually is. You may experience a range of responses to these examples, from being shocked at the language and imagery to thinking we have made too much of too little. If this book is to be of value, we would ask you to make use of what you can and let go of the rest.

The first voice is *Testimony*. This is the story of what happened, with or without judgment. It is the kind of narrative that focuses on facts and chronology but still allows us to acknowledge our emotional responses and motivations in the situation.

To make this clear we will go through this chart again telling variations on a single story. The example we will use will be adultery. The voice of testimony in our example includes the acknowledgment of how emotionally difficult the adultery was or how the end of the affair resulted in a change of behavior in similar circumstances.

The second voice is *Confession*. Here the focus is on my responsibility. There is often a specific judgment about what the narrator did or didn't do and the consequences of that internal decision which we identify as wickedness or that external circumstance we call loss.

Here the voices in our example could include a relishing of the adultery as a deliberate act or as a pleasure whose cost was high, so high that in the acting out of the affair, the thrill of flirtation was replaced with the fear of abandonment.

The third voice is *Therapy*. In this shaping of the facts, the emphasis is on understanding the relationship between what happened and what it means. In these stories we begin to look at metaphors and larger "truths" about the events: what changes when we actually acknowledge our wickedness or loss.

Here the voices of the affair might include coming to the realization that the adultery was an act of revenge on the wife's part for a past wrong by the husband. It might also be told as a set of circumstances in which two people did not make conscious decisions and consequently did not make wise ones, resulting in the breakup of their marriages.

The last voice is *Transformation,* which places its focus squarely on the action of change, on not only responding to challenge but being altered by it. In a traditional storytelling model, this would be structured as the "journey of the hero."

As an example of transformation in the adultery story, one of the parties in the affair might see that she is hurting not only her spouse but her lover and end the affair by a noble ruse, such as introducing the lover to a more suitable (and eligible) person. Another version might have one of the lovers finally leave her abusive spouse and marry the man she has been having the affair with, while volunteering to work in a women's shelter.

What is the value in taking this approach? First, it is important to understand that there is more than one way to see the story. There is more than one way to respond to the experience and its related emotions.

Oftentimes, we believe that what happened is what happened and there is only one way to recount it—the facts as we experienced them. Our entire legal system is predicated on interpreting the facts, but even when the facts are not in dispute, arriving at truth (or justice) is often a difficult proposition. Life is both subtle and more complicated than a legal judgment. In any given set of circumstances, what really happened and what it means are open to many possible constructions.

In reality, we often have mixed motives and even opposing emotional responses to a situation. Over the course of time we will see what we did or did not do in a variety of ways. What was youthful exuberance may seem in later years to be selfish and cruel. How we experience any one moment is always conditioned by our relationships and our stage of development. To quote St. Paul, "When I was a child, I spoke like a child, I thought like a child, I reasoned like a child; but when I became a man, I gave up childish ways." It is through the process of telling these difficult stories that we can face the painful realities that allow us to "give up childish ways."

Using the Continuum

We can now work through the continuum using "adultery" as an example of how we shape our stories. Our caveat is that this is not to suggest that we approve of adultery. The examples we present are not representative of our personal experience but of our thinking about a subject that is clearly a difficult one and one for which there is a rich variety of potential responses.

Another thing we should note is that the examples that follow are not complete stories. To keep the length of the book manageable, we are telling just enough of each story to give a flavor of how this particular choice might be developed. Do not get stuck on the specifics of these stories. Focus instead on the idea that each of them represents a variation on the question: how else might I shape a story about this difficult topic?

—The Seed Story—

The primary "seed story" for our example is a single se[ ]ence:
They met at a conference and they had an affair.

This is the first impulse for story. It is the nub of a tale t[ ][ ]rises
from experience or imagination and which we will shape for [ ]lling.
For the sake of our understanding the way the chart flows, [ ]e will
take the seed image and develop it both as a story of *Wi[ ][ ]dness*
and as a story of *Loss,* though in most instances you wou[ ]tend
to see it as one or the other and not both. We will begin [ ][ ]st of
these examples with the seed image and use "he" as the protagonist for the *Wickedness* examples and "she" for the examples of
the story as *Loss.* These choices are arbitrary and used for the sake
of consistency. They could have just as easily been the opposite.

As Wickedness:

They met at a conference and they had an affair. He wanted
it to happen no matter what the cost.

As Loss:

They met at a conference and they had an affair. In the end
something she valued dearly was taken away.

The seed story by itself doesn't give us much detail. It must
be further developed through a fundamental response, which for
our purposes we have identified as Denial, Guilt/Shame, Grief,
and Action. There will be four versions of the story as *Wickedness*
and another four versions of the story as *Loss* for a total of eight
variations of response. As we go through each example we will
also indicate the narrative point of view.

As Wickedness through Denial:

They met at a conference and they had an affair. It began
when she asked if there was room for another person at the

table. He said yes, and when she sat down he began a small flirtation. The flirtation led to a kiss, and because he enjoyed the kiss, he was anxious to know what would happen next. He did not think about the cost of next. It would arrive soon enough, but just then it seemed as far away as the wife who would not ask what had happened at the conference. (third person)

As Wickedness through Guilt/Shame:

I met her at a conference and we had an affair. It began with her asking me for a light for her cigarette. Although I do not approve of smoking, I wanted an opportunity to talk with her and walked out of the hall with her. I should have just given her the matches and turned my attention to the next thing on the schedule. Instead I asked her for a cigarette and began my descent into the worst kind of addiction. (first person)

As Wickedness through Grief:

I met her at a conference and we had an affair. The simple kindness of offering her a chair. She was standing there with a plate in one hand and her briefcase in the other. Had I know it would lead to the dissolution of her marriage and all the unhappiness that followed I might not have been so eager to tell her I would be glad to share my table. (first person)

As Wickedness through Action:

I met her at a conference and we had an affair. You know that is how I start this story. Not with I met you, but with I met her. It is a little fiction I offer myself, and our friends, to pro-tect your reputation and your position. Why should I use your name? You have everything to lose and I have little to gain. Though it seems like it was a long time ago, I still have the satisfaction of knowing that you once said that you couldn't live without me. (second person)

In these first four examples of response, as *Wickedn* s, the focus is on his decision to have an affair. In these next ur, as *Loss*, the focus shifts to her explanation or justification f what has happened.

As Loss through Denial:
I met him at a conference and we had an affair. It was t kind of thing that sometimes happens at conferences. M ı and women who are otherwise happy and faithful to their ouses have one drink too many and let the bounds of restra t slip. One night of trying something new and they go back what they left behind refreshed, appreciative, or in my cas satisfied that I had not harmed anyone. (first person)

As Loss through Guilt/Shame:
She met him at a conference and they had an affair. It was short, just a day or two of laughter and the delicious sense of "what if." Afterwards she was not so sure. It was not her marriage that was at risk, but her ability to pretend that it was a happy one. She hated him for that glimpse of happiness and herself for not knowing it. (third person)

As Loss through Grief:
I met him at a conference and we had an affair. He was a shark and I was one of the small fish he devoured, one or two a day. If I had known that I was not the only one, would I have cared? Would I have been more careful with my heart? He was a handsome shark. Would it have made the devouring any less hurtful? It was nothing personal. It is what sharks do. In the end, everything I valued—my dignity, my peace of mind, even my desire—was taken away from me. (first person)

As Loss through Action:
She met him at a conference and they had an affair. Her husband had done the same thing the year before. It was revenge,

pure and simple. The pictures she took were not for her pleasure but would be the pricking needles of conscience that reminded him that "what is good for the gander, is good for the goose as well." (third person)

Our story could then be further developed using one of four "voices" for each of the responses. It is in the specific choices of detail and structure that the tonality of what kind of a story this really is can be established. These four choices: *Testimony, Confession, Therapy,* and *Transformation,* when applied to the four fundamental responses will give us sixteen possible variations on the *Wickedness* side and sixteen different variations on the *Loss* side—thirty-two variations springing from our seed story in all.

Again, we will admit that the choice of *Testimony* or *Transformation* as a "voice" may be seen as arbitrary choices, but for the purpose of making clear how the story may be shaped, they will do. Learn what you will from this example and then substitute, if you wish, other characteristic voices (anger, depression, joy) in the development of your material.

For the sake of our examples, we will continue to use "he" for *Wickedness* and "she" for *Loss.* However, we will introduce variations into the stories for the structural considerations—point of view, point of entry, tone, and for the emotional arc and moral framework, which we will talk about in detail in the next chapter.

——Examples of Wickedness——

Wickedness as Denial by Testimony

They met at a conference and they had an affair. It began with her asking him if there was room at the table for another. He said yes, and when she sat down he started to flirt. The flirtation led to a kiss, and because he enjoyed her kiss, he did not think about what came next. It was four days of stealing time in each other's company and three nights in each other's arms. It did not matter that those who had traveled with him were upset by his irresponsibility. He would pay the piper some other time. She was now, and now was all he thought about. When the conference was over she'd return to her husband, and he'd return to teaching ungrateful underclassmen things they neither wanted to know nor cared about.

Wickedness as Denial in Confession

I met her at a conference and we had an affair. It began with her asking me for a light for her cigarette. Although I do not approve of smoking, I wanted an opportunity to talk with her and walked out of the hall with her. I should have just given her the matches and turned my attention to the next thing on the schedule. But little did I know that she would hand me a cigarette. Looking into her watery blue eyes, I was too polite to decline, and took it. We may have loved and lost, but every time I light up another of these coffin nails I can see the smile on her face, knowing that she wouldn't have to smoke alone.

Wickedness as Denial via Therapy

They met at a conference and they had an affair. It was careless act that made them feel as if they were still alive. / deliberate act, really, that made them feel something. Aft long marriages where feeling had moved from quick to mc bund with the surety of ice forming on the December po l, the waters stirred. Each believed they were too young to ve up risk, but longed for the kind of risk they could alway claim was accident or circumstance, rather than intentiona hurtful, or mean-spirited, when they returned to their sp ses.

Wickedness as Denial by Transformation

We met at a conference and had an affair. You w ldn't think to look at us now, happily married for over a cade, that we began with a small indiscretion. I was married at the time, but it had died long before she asked me for the time. I didn't think I was being coy when I said, how much time do you want? It just slipped out. She smiled and said, how about as long as it takes for dinner? We may have finished eating what was on the restaurant plate those many years ago, but we have yet to finish the meal.

Wickedness as Guilt/Shame by Testimony

We met at a conference and we had an affair. It was my first. It was not hers and I did not ask how many more there might have been. As many as there were conferences, perhaps. I had always wondered what it would be like. Would it be thrilling or awful? I could not have had a better teacher, for she saw in me the combination of naïveté and desire, the willingness to suspend judgment, that let her guide me through my hesitation with a swiftness and surety that made my head spin. I was always a willing pupil, and even when I thought I could no longer be surprised, I was.

Wickedness as Guilt/Shame in Confession

We met at a conference and we had an affair. I went home and tried to pretend nothing happened. My wife knew immediately. She could smell my guilt the moment I walked in the door and wasted no time asking me what had happened. I loved her and knew she deserved the truth; or perhaps I knew I was a bad liar. I told her everything. Well, almost everything. Long before the end, we were both in tears, so I skipped the part about planning to meet Lilith again.

Wickedness as Guilt/Shame via Therapy

They met at a conference and had an affair. They both understood their reasons for cheating did not justify the specific hurt that their spouses would feel and, lying in the hotel room bed, kept their counsel about why. He knew himself well enough to know that he could not and would not speak a word of this to his wife. The wife would not ask, even if she suspected, even if she was faced with the evidence of indiscretion. For the sake of the children, they would maintain the simple fiction that love could overcome bad sex or, in their case, no sex at all. He cursed himself for his weakness, but feeling a hunger for closeness that made him hard with desire, turned to the woman lying beside him and pulled her to him once again.

Wickedness as Guilt/Shame by Transformation

I met her at a conference and we had an affair. That part is easy to understand. We were telling jokes in the bar and I ordered another screwdriver. Here's the part that I have struggled with. The realization that I took it for granted. That I said it was the booze and felt that the massive hangover I had the next day was small punishment for what I had done. She offered me a delicious gift and I choked on it. It was too rich, too spicy, too meaty for my habit of living a safe life. I let her leave without telling her I didn't want to end it. That's why I'm on this plane now.

Wickedness as Grief by Testimony

I met her at a conference and we had an affair. It began with the simple act of offering her a chair. Had I known it would lead to the dissolution of her marriage and all the unhappiness that followed I night have thought twice before I motioned her over to the table. But those events would take months to play out, and at that moment I was aware only one thing, that this would be my first, last, and best chance to talk to a woman I had admired for a long time. I thought that if I didn't act now, I would regret it for the rest of my life.

Wickedness as Grief in Confession

How I came to be at this funeral is a long story. It begins simply enough. I met her at a conference and we had an affair. I never suspected that it would come to this. I hope the bastard gets the chair, I really do. If he was going to shoot someone, why her? Why not me?

Wickedness as Grief via Therapy

It was a freeing thing to do, really. I was stuck. Not that I didn't like my job and want to keep it, or at least the money it provided. When I met her at the conference, my first thought was of her legs and the way she moved in that leather skirt. I suppose I should have realized that playing with the boss's daughter was not a sensible thing to do, but I was too much of a coward to quit on my own. Unconsciously I must have realized that if I was going to go down in flames, she was a roaring bonfire. And frankly, it was worth losing the job just to see the look on his face when the elevator door opened and we were caught with my pants down and her skirt up.

Wickedness as Grief by Transformation

He met her at a conference and they set out to have an affair. He was not a man prone to rash acts, but this was one. For once in his life he would take a risk, do something unexpected. When the heart attack came at a most inopportune moment, he got his wish. He thought he was having the best sex of his life when his arm went numb and the pleasure of the groin was overtaken by the constriction of his chest. Now he lay in a hospital bed, thankful to be alive and determined to stay that way. It had been a real wake-up call. The cigarettes would have to go. So would the booze and fast food. In fact, the whole of the old life would have to go and she with it. He would miss them all.

Wickedness as Action by Testimony

We met at a conference and we had an affair. I've come to say
that it was wrong. It is better to make a clean breast of it. I
did not mean to hurt you. I won't offer excuses for what I did,
but I will ask for your forgiveness. I won't say that she seduced
me. That would be a lie. I was too willing. I doubted you and
myself, and paradoxically, the very act of betraying your trust
ended my doubt. I lay in bed after my indiscretion kr wing
that it could not go on, and I got up and left the room
intending to never see her again. To come back to y 1 and
ask you to let me make it up to you.

Wickedness as Action in Confession

I hadn't known her for a long time, but I could tell t it she
was unhappy in her marriage. She was unhappy in her x life.
She was just plain unhappy. So I asked her what woul cheer
her up and when she said, an affair, I said, that n be
arranged. I know, these things never end well, but it g ve her
the feeling that she was still attractive and that somebody
wanted her. Her husband must be dead down there, because
she really was good in the sack. If I were him, I'd have kept
her happy. So when it came time to end it, I wanted to make
her feel like it was her decision. I behaved badly. I picked a
fight with her and told her I didn't care. I told her she was a
chump for getting involved with me. It worked. She left me
and went home after the conference glad to be rid of me.

Wickedness as Action via Therapy

We met at a conference and we had an affair. Actually, nothing happened. Nothing in real life. I don't think she even
noticed me but I sure noticed her. I sat in the chair in the row
behind her and imagined what it would be like to sit next to
her. I watched her at the hotel pool and dreamt of loosening
the tie of her suit and putting lotion on the smooth mocha

curve of her back. Then one morning I was shaving and I knew that I needed help. I had left the shower running and imagined that she was in it. I could just about hear the splashing, and I thought to myself, you're in real trouble now. So I made an appointment to talk to someone. OK, I made an appointment to talk to her.

Wickedness as Action by Transformation

They met at a conference and they had an affair. It continued for a year and then for a second year. They took every chance they could find, every excuse they could offer to meet in hotels in one city or another. He grew impatient with the secrecy and lies. He wanted her to make a decision. Why should she? She had a husband that didn't care and a lover that did. And then he met Eve and knew that if he was going to have a real relationship with her, he had to end the affair. He arranged a time and place to meet, and when she opened the door, she was surprised to find not her lover but her husband sitting there.

—Examples of Loss————————

Loss as Denial by Testimony

I met him at a conference and we had an affair. He was a shark and I was one of several small fish he devoured, one or two a day. If I had known that I was not the only one, would I have cared? I think not. He was a handsome shark. Would it have made the devouring any less hurtful? It was nothing personal. It is what sharks do. In the end, everything I valued—my dignity, my peace of mind, my desire—was taken away from me. In the end I didn't care. I had wanted to be devoured, for once in my life to be relieved of responsibility. I wanted to be able to say, I had no control and what happened, happened.

Loss as Denial in Confession

I really liked him. He was a sweet man, and sweet to me. It wasn't really a mistake. Sure, he had a wife and kids. I had a husband that loved me. The moment I slipped off that dress in his hotel room, I said something good can come of this, and I was right. But you know, things have to take their course, and so we did what we did that night and went about our lives. My husband thinks this is his child and unless he's born with red hair, I suppose it's best to just let him think that.

Loss as Denial via Therapy

Did you see that movie, *Breaking the Waves?* I've lived that one. Yes, I have. The husband who says to the wife, you do what you must do to get your needs met. And me, wanting to please him and not hurt him. Me, wanting to feel alive and filled with fear that he'll be gone when I come back, every time I slip into another man's bed. Not easy, mind you. Not easy at all. But I came to an understanding of how my pleasure was his. He wanted me happy and knew that nothing made me happy like the one thing he couldn't give n .

Loss as Denial by Transformation

We met at a conference and we had an affair. Not a littl affair, but a big messy one. I don't think there was a person that conference center that didn't know exactly what we v re up to. I didn't care; for once in my life I felt as if I matt ed to someone. We sat together at every meal, at every lect . He stopped pretending he was in a separate room and mo d his suitcase into mine. I was so damned happy that I cal d the divorce lawyer before the conference was over. It wa ome-thing of a shock when I came back to the room and s that his stuff was gone. I stopped myself from saying wha fool I'd been. Just focus on what was right, I said. I was g ng to call the lawyer to stop the proceedings, when I thought to myself, why bother? It would have happened sooner or later.

Loss as Guilt/Shame by Testimony

She was one of those people who did not make conscious decisions and consequently did not make wise ones. Someone else had always told her what to do, and when she met him at the conference and he said, *Come to my room,* she did. It was not guilt that bothered her but the realization that she didn't really like him. She had not intended a life of lies. He was not an unkind man, just a needy one. So when she wanted to end their affair, she did not think he would make a scene in front of her family. He did. Now there was hell to pay. She had behaved shamefully. Her mother told her so. So did her husband as he began looking in the phone book for the name of a cheap divorce lawyer. She looked around the room, wondering who would tell her what to do now.

Loss as Guilt/Shame in Confession

Of course, it was my fault. I deserved the loss of the kids because I had set a bad example. I had been a bad wife, a bad mother. I had never even considered the embarrassment that my affair had brought to his family. Never thought that my son would be called the son of a whore. Of course he divorced me. I was lucky I wasn't in his country where by custom he could have arranged for me to be killed. I could say that I was hurt by his infidelities, but as he said, he only made love to prostitutes, not married women.

Loss as Guilt/Shame via Therapy

They met at a conference and they had an affair. She had been in love with him for a long time and wanted, no, willed it to happen. In the office they had flirted a little. He had taken her to lunch and once, after pulling in a multi-million dollar

account, they shared a congratulatory kiss in the elevat r. She
knew he was married and thought that if she could st get
him to see her for who she was, not as his pal or co-v rker,
he'd understand how much he meant to her. Why he lid it,
didn't matter now. She had him in her bed and he was appy
to play by her rules. She liked that. More than she t ught
she would. And suddenly she realized it wasn't him t t she
was in love with, it wasn't the dream of having a har some
man to wake up in bed with or to bring her roses; it was the
idea that he would do her bidding. She blushed at the
thought. In the end, it made little difference whether he
stayed or left. There could always be another.

Loss as Guilt/Shame by Transformation

In those days I went through men like some women go
through a shoe store. Even as I was trying on one, my eye had
fixed on another, the one I really wanted. Except for Byron.
He was the last one. We met at a conference and had an affair.
When it was over he was weeping. I didn't or perhaps couldn't
care that I had broken that sweet man's heart and put him
into his car with a breezy kiss, telling him that I'd be a fond
memory to share with his drinking buddies back at home.
When I heard that the car had run off the road I had to stop
and ask myself what I was doing. It doesn't matter whether
I killed him or not, I had put him behind the wheel as if it
made no difference.

Loss as Grief by Testimony

Things were better now. It had been touch and go for a long
time. Her husband was not surprised that she had an affair.
What bothered him was that she might have loved the other
man. Sex, that could be understood, but not love. But in spite
of his protestations, he remained detached from every emotion but anger while her lover celebrated her at every turn. As

much as she wanted her husband to change, it became clear that he would not, and she filed the papers. After the divorce, she realized that every time she saw her lover she was reminded of her husband. The two were linked in her emotions and she could not let go of the one without letting go of the other. In the end she sent him away as well in hopes that once alone, truly alone, she could discover how to love herself.

Loss as Grief in Confession

We met at a conference and had an affair. It was my first. I don't think there was a person at that conference center that didn't know exactly what we were up to. I didn't care; for once in my life I felt as if I mattered to someone. We sat together at every meal, at every lecture. He stopped pretending he was in a separate room and moved his suitcase into mine. I was so damned happy that I called the divorce lawyer before the conference was over. So it was a real shock when I came into the room and saw that his stuff was gone. My diamond necklace too. What a fool I'd been. I couldn't look my husband in the face when he asked me what the hell was going on. I didn't even try to explain the divorce, I just took the token settlement he offered and decided that I'd never trust a man again.

Loss as Grief via Therapy

After the affair came the divorce, and only then did she understand that it was not only a marriage that was ended but her identity as wife and her hopes of being a mother. By the time she could enter a stable relationship again, she would be too old to have children without risk. She could try now, as a single mother, but her own shaky sense of self told her it would be a struggle. And so she grieved not only what had been lost to the pleasure of the affair but that which had always remained as a possibility within the marriage. In the end she was alone and had to discover how to live with herself.

Loss as Grief by Transformation

She met him at a conference and they set out to have an affair. He was not a man prone to rash acts, and this was one. She appreciated his willingness to take a risk and was hoping for something unexpected. The heart attack came at a most inopportune moment. She was having the best sex of her life when his face knotted up in pain and he clutched his chest. Now he lay in a hospital bed, and she was preparing to go to her next keynote. She sent him flowers and a card wishing him a speedy recovery. She made a note to herself to d_ _s the paramedic had suggested: take a refresher course in C _ and buy another bottle of aspirin.

Loss as Action by Testimony

In the end he forgave me. We met at a conference and _e had an affair. It did not matter why, or who started it, th_ result was the same. I was in love with him, and he was n_ rried. We swore that it was over after the second night. He _as in tears, unable to perform, and I held him like a child, _lling him that he should go back to his wife and forget al _bout me. Once he left I was in tears at the thought of no_ _eing him again. Six months later, he was standing at the d_ _r and I put good sense aside as easily as I asked him in. But y our third bedding, he was once again paralyzed with gui_ _nd I needed to get my psychic house in order. I told him _ _ had to leave. I told him he couldn't call me or see me until he left his wife. He begged. This time I was firm. It took three months of me hanging up the phone every time he called before the copy of the divorce papers arrived. Then I called him and asked if he wanted some company.

Loss as Action in Confession

I was at the age where the doubt settles in. Two children and no matter what I did, my belly remained a curve. I did not think anyone would find me attractive. We met at a conference, and we had an affair. Not at the conference. I did not think he even noticed me there and was quite surprised when he leaned over in the crowded bar to make the suggestion. *I'm married,* I said, and he removed his hand from where it had been resting. No, it was after that, when he wrote to apologize, that the seed of desire, once planted, bloomed. I courted him as earnestly as any suitor would her heart's delight and worked out a circumstance where we could be together. I wanted to know that I was still beautiful, and he would tell me what I longed to hear.

Loss as Action via Therapy

I met him at a conference and we had an affair. Three times a year over the space of two years I went to him and said, use me. I wanted to be scared and thrilled and helpless. I wanted to make violent love. Have him bite me. Claw his back. Leave marks. I know that what I wanted with him was what I could not say or do with my husband. He was happy to oblige. He liked being in charge. Then just before Christmas he came to see me. It was the first, last, only time he had been in my town. We met that afternoon in an old hotel, making love in a room so cold that we could write our names on the frosty windows. He wrote, leave your husband, your job, this town. And I wrote, goodbye. I know when it's over, when it gets too serious to continue. It's when they think that this is everyday and not the reward we give ourselves for surviving the everyday.

Loss as Action by Transformation

They met at a conference and had an affair. She was afraid that her husband would find out and kill one or both of them. He asked her why she stayed. She said she had no place to go. He wrote the name and phone number of a women's shelter on a card. She did not think she'd hear from him again. One day he called. She asked how he got her number. He said that it didn't matter. His question was: why was she still there? Then he offered to take her to the shelter. She didn't think of what she was leaving or even pack a bag when she walked out the door. It took months to let go of the feeling that she had lost not only a house but a life. Two years later she was still at the shelter, not as a resident but as staff. She was fond of saying that sometimes what we think of as a sin is the first step to salvation.

· · ·

So there you have thirty-two variations on a single seed image: *they met at a conference and they had an affair.* In working through the chart, it becomes clear that in some instances the distinction between one "voice" and another may be fine and the changing of a few words or the point of view may suggest positioning a story at one or another place along the chart.

What is important is not *where* we place the story but the fact that in every case there is a conscious decision about *how we are shaping the material.*

Select a story from your life. Using a piece of paper or a journal, take it through a portion of the wickedness-loss chart. Decide first whether it is fundamentally a story of wickedness (internal choice) or of loss (external circumstance). For whichever polarity you choose, next identify what you believe your response was: denial, guilt/shame, grief, or action? Once you make that choice, try to identify the voice you have used to tell yourself and others that story. Is it told as testimony, confession, therapy, or transformation? Write out the progression of that story.

Now think about how you would tell that story in terms of the other polarity. If you see it as wickedness, try reframing it as loss. If you see it as loss, in what way could it be articulated as wickedness?

Now go through the same progression, being mindful of other choices around the responses and the voice that you could use to tell it. If you now see it as guilt, can you see it as grief? If the voice of the experience is one of confession, can you tell it as transformation? Write out a progression of your choice for that story.

Compare the two versions.

Overarching
Structural Elements

What really counts is to strip the soul naked.
Painting or poetry is made as we make love,
a total embrace, nothing held back.
—Joan Miro

We have dealt with tone (comedy/tragedy), point of view, point of entry, and the wickedness-loss continuum in our considera-tion of the structural elements. In many ways, the two that remain, the emotional arc and moral framework, are the most difficult aspects to work with. It is here that our ownership of the story is manifest. By setting these final two in place, the teller makes clear his or her personal relationship to the material.

The choice for comedy or tragedy is not really about the teller's personal view. It is about the way the teller wants to craft an invitation for the audience to enter the difficult story. Comedy is often a way of holding the material at bay. It has the benefit of giving the audience the opportunity, through laughter, to get comfortable before having to come to an understanding of diffi-culty. But it can also be a crutch that enables a teller to deny her own feelings while attempting to deal with the topic. It can also be a way for the teller to disguise pain as "the tears of the clown."

Tragedy has a more direct appeal but allows its own kind of distancing in the creation and resolution of tension. It can be a dramatic choice to amplify emotions. It can be a means to create larger-than-life experiences. It can facilitate a kind of substitution in which external events displace or replace the more intimate and internal experience.

Likewise, the choice for point of view often has more to do with the listener than the teller. The choices of point of view are often about distancing the teller from the story even as she invites the listener into the story. Do you want the listener to identify you with the particulars of the material? Do you place yourself at the center of the story or at the edge? Are you narrating from inside the experience or as an observer?

The shift in the decision-making process begins with the wickedness-loss continuum. Here the teller takes into account his own sense of what the story means and how to shape the specific content. Now that the decisions about how the listener will be invited into the story via tone and point of view have been made, the real shaping of the story begins. Begins but does not end, for the framework of the wickedness-loss continuum is just that, a framework, not the finished structure.

It is in the crafting of the emotional arc and the setting of the moral framework that the teller must complete the story. Here is where she must decide how she feels about the material and how she wants the audience to feel. It is in these two components that she must make a personal commitment to the meaning of the story.

—Emotional Arc—————————————

It is essential to know that the emotional arc of the story is not the same as plot. The plot of a story is what happens. It is the order of progression. It is a chronology, a way to manage time. The emotional arc is not about what happens but how we feel about what happens.

One way of understanding that notion is found in this description of the blues: "In the first verse I use the knife o cut the bread, in the second verse I use the knife to shave, in tl third verse I use the knife to cut my lying lover's throat. It's th same knife, but how it's used is what changes." And how e feel about the knife changes as well. (Unfortunately, we don't r nember who first said it, so some blues man will once ag in go uncredited for his genius.)

Suppose you are a lawyer representing a client in a p oduct liability case. You are working with a set of facts abo how your client came to his difficulty. The lawyer represent g the defendant will present a very different interpretation of the same facts. What is the difference between the facts? They are the same facts. What is different is how those facts are seen and how seeing them that way changes one's conclusion. In presenting the facts to a jury, you want to do it in a way that encourages them to be sympathetic to your client. To do so, you must invite them to feel what your client feels, to craft the presentation of facts in such a way that as the jury hears the story, its emotional arc takes them closer to your client's experience and feelings.

A well-crafted emotional arc may parallel the plot of the story; conversely, it may stand in opposition to it. As an example, the following story has little or no plot in a traditional sense. It presents facts and relies on the listener to arrive at an emotional response to those facts. The story is focused not on what is said but on what is not said. The narrator is outside the story; there is no hero with whom to identify. Yet this combination of elements provides a wonderful platform to let the emotional arc work.

Slaughter House

I lived in a meat-packing town.

The meat-packing plant at one time ran three kills: one for sheep, hogs, and cattle. The end of the road for the lot of them was the stainless-steel world of the slaughterhouse.

It was a gravity plant. The animals were herded out of trucks, up chutes, and onto the fifth floor. There they were held in pens, then led to the killing floor. They entered at the top on the hoof and left out the bottom wrapped in plastic.

Inside the plant, everything was stainless steel and ceramic. Workers wore white smocks and small hard hats, steel-toed shoes and steel-meshed gloves. Everything was wet and reeked of death: blood, fat, shit, urine, guts, half-digested corn and hay, digestive juices, and the sweat of the workers—everyone working hard to keep up with the line.

Gravity moves an object at thirty-three feet per second.

Of the three species killed there, only the cattle knew what was coming. If a pig got loose on the kill, it would wander around eating bits of pig flesh off the floor until it was herded back on the line and slaughtered.

Sheep never wandered off the kill. They were led up the chute at the back of the plant by a Judas goat. The goat returned, but the sheep didn't.

They were herded into small holding pens, twenty in each. And then the knocker arrived. The knocker was the guy who killed the animals. He held a mechanism that, when placed next to the head of an animal, propelled a steel rod into the brain—powered by a .22 caliber shell. The sheep stood there chewing while the knocker walked up to each one and killed them. The last would be calmly standing in a pen of dead sheep, and then it'd get knocked.

Cattle, as I said before, know exactly what was happening. Left in the trucks at the back of the plant, they moan and howl and shit all over themselves. They can smell death. The truck backs up to the chute, the doors fling open, and three workers herd them out using electric cattle prods as long as a man's arm. They herd them up the chute until they reach a holding pen. Above the pen is an interconnected network of aluminum catwalks.

All the time, the cattle are howling and moaning and fighting not to go.

Now many of these are beef cattle or steers, raised for the purpose of finding their way onto our dinner plates. But others are dairy cows who've outlived their economic utility and been sold off to the plant. They've lived many years with people, have names, and are accustomed to the touch of human hands.

Once in the pens, workers enter above on the catwalks. Using cattle prods, they herd three at a time into a steel chute. The doors slam shut, automatically. The cattle are packed in so tight that they can hardly move. Then up comes the knocker. He knocks the first. Hot blood and brains spray out like a geyser as it drops to the deck. Blood and shattered bone are everywhere.

The knocker is covered in blood and gore. The second struggles to stick its head under the ass of the dead cow in front of it . . .

Knock.

It drops dead.

Then the third.

Dead.

The chute tilts up by hydraulics and the cattle slide into the shackling pit. Even though they're dead, they're still kicking like mad as if trying to get free. The shackler hooks a chain around the leg of each cow, who is immediately pulled into the air and drawn over the bleeding pit.

In the bleeding pit, every thirty seconds a worker jams a long knife into the throat of a cow. He plunges the knife in as far as he can reach, right up to his shoulder. When he withdraws it, a torrent of blood flows out.

At any given moment, twenty dead cows hang over the floor of the bleeding pit. In the middle is a drain. Above it, standing in anywhere from six to eighteen inches of blood, a younger worker rakes free the blood clots to keep the drain from clogging.

Twenty hours a day, six days a week, the blood keeps flowing.

Now sometimes a cow gets loose on the kill. It goes crazy. Knocking over workers, breaking machinery, trying desperately to get out. Everything stops. The floor is cleared and a worker enters with a rifle. The cow stands exhausted and terrified. The worker aims and fires. The cow drops to the floor. And within minutes the kill is working again.

The plant runs like this twenty hours a day, six days a week:

2 head of beef a minute

120 an hour

2,400 a day in two ten-hour shifts

14,400 a week

nearly 750,000 head of beef slaughtered a year.

The only woman who works on the kill has the last job on the line. She cuts off the tails. And when the last carcass comes down the line, she cuts off its tail and yells down to the floor below: "All dead!"

The workers below send the cry down to eac floor below them until the entire plant echoes with *All d d! All dead! All dead!*

They bang their knives against steel and cheer.

If you eat meat, I did your killing for you.

TIM: "Slaughter House" appears in a longer performance piece entitled *Esker*. It is roughly a meditation on the landscape of southern Minnesota and my own life experience, part real, part imagined. "Slaughter House" sets aside another story entitled "Roger Tollofson." Roger works at the plant and is a WWII veteran. As a pair, they work as a story of spiritual redemption—as unlikely as that seems from reading "Slaughter House" when it stands alone.

Over the past twelve years, I've performed a number of short and full-length pieces in which I construct arcs of spoken-word lyrics that are held together by shared or complementary images. I tend not to be very interested in narrative as a rhetorical device. I like to think that the relationship between the performer and listener, if sufficiently dynamic, allows for the creation of a vicarious (for the listener) and imagined (for the performer) narrative context, within which the details find a home in the lives of each.

Please read 'Slaughter House' out loud, and preferably in front of someone else or even a group. It was first performed extemporaneously. I only wrote it down because I had to work with a director. It works best off the tongue rather than off the page.

TIM HERWIG *is a storyteller, writer, and performance artist living in Chicago.*

• • •

As we said, there is no hero in this story. Not even a central character. The narrator is external. Much of the narration is a recitation of facts about the slaughter house. It is the accumulation of those carefully chosen facts that builds tension.

There is an unspoken sense of judgment from the start. At first, that judgment seems to be about the nature of the meat-packing plant, but with the last line it is turned on the listener, with an implied question about us. Whether the listener is a carnivore or a vegetarian, the emotional arc of the story takes us from neutrality to an emotionally charged resolution.

. . .

It is difficult to generalize about how to construct an emotional arc. They are as individual as the stories we tell. It is much easier to see how it works in relationship to a particular story. The emotional arc of "Slaughter House" is specific to that story. While Loren's first story, "By the Grace of God," ends by shifting the listener's frame of reference much as Tim does in "Slaughter House," it arrives at its destination in a very different way. Loren assumes the listener will identify with the narrator's circumstances and come to an appreciation of the meaning of the story in the process.

Like the point of entry, the crafting of the emotional arc is a critical process. Do you want your listeners to be comfortable or discomforted? Do you want them to have a sense of completion or of ambiguity? Do you want the listeners to identify with the characters in the story or with the situation? Often the difference between one outcome and another is in the framing of the emotional arc.

We usually begin shaping the emotional arc by creating a sense of identity between the listener and some crucial element—character, subject matter, or narrator, for instance. The listener should be able to recognize what is happening. They may see it as an experience they have had or could have. They may feel a sense of familiarity with the situation: *I've been there. I've felt that.* Loren's "By the Grace of God" invites the listener to recognize the narrator's experience through the description of being asked for money: *Oh, I've had that happen to me. I know what that feels like.*

We develop the arc in relationship to the plot. This can be closely linked or not. It can be a fast link, built upon action, revelation, or surprise. It can be slow, built incrementally through details that let the listener move from the initial recognition to a deeper, more satisfying emotional response. Conversely, the emotional arc can stand in contrast to what is happening, as would be the case in a story based on a response of denial. It can have a giddy romantic quality or a sobering progression. We know from experience that however you choose to develop the arc, it can and should be consciously crafted.

After the initial identification with the narrator's situation in "By the Grace of God," the listener is invited to suspend his judgment of Tommy the Wino's character while two images are presented that draw the listener into a world that he may not know. The first is the harsh reality of the liquor store, the second is the low-key humor of the sharing of the bottle. In the process, the listener should become increasingly comfortable with Tommy as a person rather than as a caricature.

The final function of the emotional arc is the resolution. It should bring our story to an end in such a way as to have the listener feel that it is complete, that it satisfies a need to have a full experience of image and text. This is the difference between a story and an anecdote. A story is chosen and as such has a particular shape and meaning. An anecdote is still raw, not necessarily understood, shaped, or satisfying.

One element of shaping a personal anecdote into a meaningful story is that we are able to see the end of the story. We choose to have it stop at a particular place. We understand how it should feel and can construct the narrative to arrive at that conclusion. In the process of crafting an emotional arc, we can share that feeling with the listener.

At the end of "By the Grace of God," the resolution of the emotional arc comes with the statement: "You shared a bottle with me. You're one of us." In that statement, the audience is invited to consider the common ground that Tommy, the narrator, and themselves as listeners all share. In this case the resolution of the arc and the conclusion of the story are simultaneous. There is no need to say anything else afterwards.

This is not always the case. In telling some stories, the resolution of the emotional arc arrives before the end of the plot. In a classic sense, what follows is the denouement, which ties up the loose ends and gives listeners a chance to return to their world. Stepping away from the emotional conclusion before you get to the narrative conclusion is a reasonable choice. The conscious decision about what is told is critical. You must be willing to look at every element of the story, both the structural considerations of what you say and the emotional or moral framework of how it is said.

─Moral Framework──────────────

Each of us comes to a moral framework for stories based on our personal perspective. If we begin with the beliefs of right and wrong that we hold closest, they usually reflect our religious background and upbringing. For some, it is the Ten Commandments or the Golden Rule. For others, it reflects the study of ethics, philosophy, theology, or psychology. For still others, the sense of "ought" and "should" is tempered by the experience of therapy or a Twelve Step program. We may articulate deeply held be efs or we may choose to voice skepticism, to "play the Devil's adv :ate." We would argue, as we have throughout this book, that o view is not necessarily better than another, but that *making a co scious decision about what view you hold is critical.*

Because a particular topic may be harder for you to add ,ss, or for the listener to hear, it is all the more important that you have a clear sense of what is at stake. Even if you want to use an ambiguous or amoral framework to let the listener enter the difficult story and come to his or her own conclusion about what is right or wrong, it must be consciously chosen and carefully framed. It cannot be arrived at by accident. As an example, here is a story about a very difficult topic, suicide.

LOREN NIEMI

The Rug

It took a long time before anyone noticed something was wrong, and a bit longer before the first complaint was made. They thought it might be some food gone bad, or a pet who had had an accident. But there was no pet, and no one answered the knock at the door. The messages piled up, and all the while the smell got worse.

When they finally opened the door, the body had been there for a long time.

Too cheap to replace what was a new and supposedly stain-resistant carpet, they bleached and shampooed it until the deep red had faded to a slighter shade of pale. Then they rented the apartment out at a substantially discounted price and said nothing about the unfortunate incident that had prompted the sudden vacancy.

But once the carpet had tasted blood, it hungered for more.

They were a couple possessed of dreams. He wanted to be an artist. No, he was an artist, what he wanted was to be a very well-known and well-paid artist. She was more modest, wanting only to do some good, to fulfill a need, to be free of the dreary nether world that afforded them this nondescript suburban apartment with its bland suburban view. She worked in data entry, punching in numbers, all day, every day, day in and day out.

At night he would paint pictures of car wrecks, crumpled fields of shiny metal and bent chrome. She would stand with her bare feet planted in the soft rug, staring out the window at the empty swimming pool and thinking nothing focused or complete, just feeling something was absent from her life.

They began to bicker, without the formality of angry words, or maybe not so much bicker as stake out emotional territory.

They would leave clues and make statements without having to actually speak to one another. He put a picture of Princess Di on the wall and scrawled *As famous as* in bold strokes beneath it. She countered with one of Mother Teresa, *Better goodness than beauty* written in a small tentative script, then crossed it out and replaced it with *So pure of heart!!*

His paintings got bigger, taking up ever-larger sections of wall. The dialogue about who they would become was measured with Post-it Notes and clippings that soon crowded out even those declarations of disaster.

She often lay on the rug, listening to the worsted silence punctuated by tuneless humming. She felt little except the comfort of the carpet, like so many tiny arms supporting the weight of her sadness.

One night she picked up the stencil knife with it sharp thin blade, the easy grip handle. Tracing the line of he veins, the long line of life, tracing pulse wanting to break ou of the dreary confinement, she made her mark. His newest painting of a truck wrapped around a concrete pillar neede some more red running down the door.

The red flowed so easily.

She lay on the floor looking at the painting with ; thin trickle of life running down the wall.

As she sank into darkness, the rug drank its fill.

Loren has told this story many times, usually presentin t as a "ghost" story. As a creepy tale, the ambiguous moral f ming serves its function very well. A few years ago, however, he happened to tell it at the Sharing the Fire Conference in Boston and afterward was approached by an obviously upset woman who asked how he could make suicide so attractive. He tried to explain that he did not think the story was crafted to make suicide attractive at all. This answer did not satisfy her. When Loren inquired about what she found objectionable within the story, it became clear that the real issue was not the story itself but the disturbing emotional association she made between it and her own experience of the suicide of a family member.

She wanted a different story with a different moral framework. To be satisfactory to her, it would clearly condemn the taking of one's own life. She did not want to be reminded of tragedy and loss. The fact was that even if Loren told the story in a way that met her need for moral clarity, it would not bring back her lost one. Changing the story or adding cautionary notes might ease her pain, but would it serve the needs of the rest of the audience or the story?

The great danger of the moral framework is that sometimes we are so sure of our view that we want to preach—either to the choir or to the sinners. Preaching is for those who have already converted. Preaching to the choir reminds them that they are on the right path. Preaching to the sinners seldom produces converts. No one repents until they are ready to preach themselves. If we want to make converts of the sinners, we need to demonstrate the advantages of the right path by example.

After this encounter, Loren wondered if the woman would have spoken to him about her response to the subject if he had told a story that had agreed with or reinforced her own moral position. In telling a story that stood at odds with her expectations, he invited her not only to consider what her position was but to engage him in a dialogue about the meaning of the tale.

Within the ambiguous moral framework of the story, Loren crafts two experiences: the first is a hallmark of many suicides—the evocation of the seemingly casual provocation with which they occur. The other is the invitation for the listeners to consider what their feelings might be about the taking of one's life. In leaving the interpretation open, he trusts the listener to be able to come to a judgment about the material.

In reading the first draft of this book, Elizabeth remarked that if it was a ghost story in the traditional sense, she felt the story was somehow incomplete. It should have a third segment, for we know that in the folktale world, things often happen in threes. So here is Loren's addition of a third part to give it the sensibility of a traditional story:

They had to replace the rug this time. A man was hired to come in and tear it out. He cut it into sections and rolled it up. It was stiff with blood, and he cursed and groaned as he pulled it away from the places where it was stuck to the floor. The rug knew nothing of its destiny when it was loaded into the bed of the pickup. What it knew was a familiar thirst, and it exerted whatever will it had to satisfy that craving. In the cab, the workman began to think that it was a shame that the whole rug had to go to the dump when just one section of it was ruined.

Even as the thought of taking home the good half grew, his eyes fluttered. It had been a long day after a long night. When the police arrived, they found the truck wedged between the pillar and the steel rail that should have kept it from hitting the same. A thin line of red ran down the door from the shattered glass of the driver's window. The steering wheel with the faulty airbag pressed against the man's chest. The back window was also shattered, and a section of it had fallen into the cab. The man was slumped, bleeding profusely, across it.

By time they got him out of the cab, the rug was soaked red and satisfied once more.

What does it do to the moral framework when Loren adds this third section? If it makes it more like a traditional tale, does it make the story any easier to hear? Is it easier to put aside? Does it let him, as a teller, or you, as a listener, off the emotional hook when it moves more firmly into the tradition of the ghost story? Does it lessen or increase the morally ambiguous tension inherent in the other version?

These are important questions to ask in shaping the moral framework of a story. Do you want to illustrate a specific lesson, as many fables do, or leave the lesson open to interpretation, as many parables do? Think about the stories in the Zen, Sufi, or

Hassidic traditions. They rise out of spiritual principle but often contain ambiguous meanings. Their moral frameworks are layered so listeners at different stages of spiritual study will understand different but appropriate meanings.

As elements are added to or subtracted from the story, the moral center shifts. This is the case with all stories but needs to be carefully considered in the difficult one. Consider how Elizabeth develops her sense of what is required for a true sympathetic understanding and sense of justice in this story:

ELIZABETH ELLIS

Political Prisoner

It was Lawton, Oklahoma. I was visiting the community college to teach workshops to low-income parents about the importance of their family stories and how their children would benefit from them. When the workshop was over for the day, my friend Steve Kardaleff asked me if I wanted to go over to Fort Sill. "What's at Fort Sill?" I asked.

"The stockade," he replied. "Geronimo was held a prisoner there for many years. They say he was never still. He paced in his cell until he wore a path in the stone floor."

I said, "No, I don't want to look at that. It would be too painful."

"Well," he said, "we could go and see where Geronimo is buried."

I said, "That sounds less painful. At least the man was dead by then. Let's go there."

I figured I did not want to go to Geronimo's grave empty-handed. I asked Steven to stop at a convenience store we passed. I went in and asked for a couple of bags of rolling tobacco. The guy behind the counter gave me a hard time. He said, "You don't exactly look like someone who rolls their own." I just laughed and shined him on.

We pulled into a parking lot facing a long row of evergreen trees. Since their branches reached the ground, we had to walk all the way to the end of the row before we could see the cemetery. As we turned round the last tree, there before us stretched row after row after row of graves. On each one was a concrete cross. Row after long straight row of white concrete crosses. Carved into them were names like Morning Dove and White Bear. The names looked so out of place on those white concrete crosses.

We followed the rows into the middle of the cemetery. In the center was a large mound of concrete. That was all—a large mound of concrete. There was no sign that might tell you what this man did in his lifetime. There were not even the customary dates of birth and death. Only one word: GERONIMO. Why, that wasn't even the man's name. They had only called him that because his first attack had occured on St. Gerome's Day.

I stood and looked at the grave. I could not believe what I was seeing. Perhaps somewhere deep inside me I could understand what would make them want to hold him prisoner all those years. Perhaps I understood the fear they had that told them it was too dangerous to free him. But why did they have to disrespect the man in this way? Anger boiled up inside me. I thought, *When the man was dead he could be no more threat to them. Why did they have to treat him with such disrespect? What would it have cost them to return him to his people? Or barring that, to bury him as his people would have? What would it have cost them?*

I bent down toward the edge of the great mound of concrete and began to make my little gift of tobacco. That is when I saw it, glittering in the grass. I pulled it up out of the grass and held it on the palm of my hand to look at it more closely. It was a handcuff key.

In that moment I knew two things clearly. The first was they were using convicts for the upkeep of this cemetery. Since I was standing in Oklahoma, the state with the largest Native population, I wondered how many of the men cleaning these graves could legitimately be thought of as political prisoners.

The other was that their disrespect had been great, but mine had been greater. I had been unwilling to look at the man's pain. Perhaps that is the greatest disrespect we can pay anyone: to be unwilling to look at their pain. If they could live it, I could look at it. Perhaps it was the very least I could do. The least I can do.

So, the next day when the workshops were over, Steven drove me to Fort Sill. We sat a long time looking at the stone walls and stone ceiling of that cell, but I spent a longer time looking at the worn stone floor and weeping.

No one had told us that they closed the campus of the community college on Saturday afternoon. So we were surprised to see the padlock on the gate at the entrance. I could look across the fence and see my car in the parking lot, being held a political prisoner. Steven offered to climb the fence to try to find a security guard.

He was gone awhile. When he returned he said, "There's nobody in there at all."

I said, "I really need to get home to Dallas. I can't wait till Monday to go home!" We sat in the front seat of Steven's pickup truck and looked at the fence.

All of a sudden he said, "I think I can get that sec on of the fence down." Steven may be a Macedonian-Am ican, but he is also an Oklahoma good ol' boy. There are ways going to be tools in the back of his pickup truck.

He climbed the fence a second time and begar disassembling a section of the fence. I began looking for the police. I may be a storyteller, but I wasn't sure I would be able to come up with a story about this that would satisfy them.

When Steven had the section of fence on the ground, I drove my car over it and out onto the street. Then I held that piece of the fence upright while he put it back together. I drove home to Dallas.

A few hours later, I took the exit off the freeway that would lead me to my house. They were standing there. Right where they always are. Men with bedrolls at their feet. Some of them hold signs that say, WILL WORK FOR FOOD. Some say, HELP A VET. Occasionally a brazen one will hold out a sign that simply says, NEED A BEER.

I had seen their bedrolls before. I had even seen their signs. I had never really seen them. We are always careful not to look at them. But I had Geronimo's handcuff key on the dashboard of my car. So I looked right at them, and smiled. I smiled as though I were looking into the face of a friend.

As I turned the corner, I realized I *had* been looking into the face of a friend. But that wasn't possible. We don't know people who stand on the street and hold signs. But I knew that face.

I turned around and got back on the freeway. I got off at the next exit so I could come back in front of them. It was him. My mind went reeling back fifteen years, when I had inherited a grandchild to raise. This man had edited a local magazine and invented errands for me to run so I could buy diapers and formula.

I turned the corner again. This time I pulled into the gas station. I threw open the passenger-side car door and yelled his name.

His head whipped around. He took a couple of steps in my direction. I called his name again. His face broke open in a grin, and he started running toward me. Just as he reached my car, he stopped.

"Get in!" I called.

"No," he said.

"Get in!" I called again.

"No," he said. "You'd never get the smell out of your upholstery."

"I don't care," I said fiercely. "I'll burn it if I have to. Get in."

I took him to my home. While he was in the shower, I raided my grandson's closet for clean clothes. I put a meal on the table. I let him eat his fill before I asked him for his story.

I am not afraid of giant bugs that devour Cleveland. Nothing Vincent Price ever starred in scared me. But what I heard from this man was truly frightening.

After the magazine folded, he had gone back to counseling drug addicts in a federally funded program. It had been hard work, but he felt like he was making a difference.

Then they received word that they had lost their funding. Each of them had begun looking for other jobs. He had interviewed for several, always being one of the three finalists. Always being called back for the second interview. Then he would never hear from them again.

Other people began to find jobs, but he was not afraid. There was still time. Then the funding ended, but he still was not afraid. He had unemployment and savings to fall back on. He was sure something would turn up soon. He was still going on those second interviews. But now he called to check on the job when he did not hear back from them. He noticed when he did so that their attitudes toward him had changed. They would be curt, almost to the point of being rude.

First the unemployment ran out, then the savings. Finally a day came when the rent was due, and he did not have it. When he was evicted, he put his dogs in the car and took them to the S.P.C.A. He begged the lady behind the counter to keep them together. "They've been together since they were puppies," he told her. "If you split them up, they might grieve themselves to death." He knew who was likely to grieve himself to death.

He lived in his car for a while. Then the oil pump went out. One day while he was out trying to find something to eat, they hauled his car away. Now he was truly on the street.

He found out quickly why people would rather be on the street than go to a homeless shelter. "They are cruel places," he said. "When the people there discover you have an education, they hate you even more than they did already. And when the people who run them discover you have an education, they can't believe you would ever let yourself get into a situation like this."

A worker at one of the soup kitchens told him if you had been homeless for more than a year you could apply to the housing authority for Section 8 housing. So he went over to fill out the paperwork. The woman was very helpful, he said. But he could tell she had never been homeless. She told him to come back in just three weeks. If she had ever been homeless, she would never have described it as "just" three weeks.

He waited out the time sleeping in parks and under bridges. He returned to her office with a heart full of hope. Instead of the friendly smile he had seen before, he was met with a face of fury. "You lied to me," she spat at him. "You nearly got me fired."

"What are you talking about?" he asked her.

"I tried to help you and I nearly lost my job. You aren't eligible to receive any kind of assistance. You're a convicted felon."

"A felon!" he gasped. "Why, I've never been arrested in my whole life. I've never even gotten a speeding ticket. What are you talking about?"

She continued to berate him. He begged her to explain. He begged her to show him his record. She flipped on her computer and showed him the screen. There was his name, his Social Security number, and the notation that he was a convicted felon.

He stared at the screen, and then he started to sob. She called security. They led him from the building, still sobbing.

It would be months before he would find out what had happened. Another man—with the same first, middle, and last names, born in the same month of the year, even on the same day of the month, but with birth years nearly two decades apart—was the felon. Someone sitting at the computer had been in a hurry to go to lunch. They had not checked the Social Security numbers. That one computer error had cost him life as he knew it.

I do angry very well. I said, "I'll get this straightened out in no time." It was ten days before the legal clinic for the indigent could see us. They said, "We only deal with criminal cases. Your friend did not really commit a crime so we can't help him."

Civil legal help for the indigent is even more diff ılt to come by. We would have to wait almost three weeks ır the appointment. They told us, "A felony is a criminal offense. We only deal with civil matters. It is outside the scope of our office to help you." My friend had fallen through the cracks.

Several more weeks would go by before someone would suggest to me the law clinic at Southern Methodist University. We drove there and spent a very frustrating quarter of an hour trying to explain the situation to a young lady behind the desk. All the time we were talking, a man was standing near the water cooler, listening.

After a while he stepped toward us. He said, "I am a professor in the law school here. I would really like to talk about your problem to the students in my ethics class. Would that be okay with you?"

My friend said, "Yes, if it will help you any, I don't mind if you talk about it."

I said, "You can talk about it all you want. But it's going to cost you! You are a professor here. That means you must also be a lawyer. You can fix this. For God's sake, do so."

"Of course I will," he replied. He thought it would be a simple matter to tend to. But it would be weeks before the paperwork was completed, even with his position and hotshot law degree.

My friend is not the same person he used to be. He is jittery and spooks easily. He did not return to counseling drug addicts. That was too demanding emotionally. He has an efficiency apartment. He took a job at the community college helping people make career decisions. It is calmer work. He takes a great interest in helping them consider all the possibilities.

He called me up not long ago and asked me to come over. He said he had a surprise he wanted to show me. It was a kitten. I would not have believed that nine ounces of black and white fur could make anyone so happy. If this were a made-up story, I would tell you that he let me name the kitten and that I called it Geronimo. But this is not a made-up story. The kitten has a stupid name. His name is Sport.

I clipped that handcuff key on my key ring. It is still there. If they can live it, we can look at it. It is the least we can do.

If the focus of the last three chapters of this book has been on technical aspects of structuring difficult stories, we do so to provide tools to help inform the content. But the core issue is not how you arrange the story, but what the story is. Elizabeth is telling a story that means something to her. It burns with the desire to understand and share an experience that is both personal and universal. There is a problem that must be understood. There is something that needs to be spoken. She has a clear moral view and she means to share it. Nothing can replace that sense of urgency about wanting to share with another the righting of a wrong.

If we can tell these stories, you can too. It happens when you look at the difficult stories and decide to tell them truthfully and artfully. It is not a matter of inspiration or genius, it is a matter of trust, permission, and ownership. It is a matter of practice. It is a matter of working and reworking a story until every aspect comes into alignment and does what it must to be what it is. As Thomas Edison said, "Genius is one percent inspiration and ninety-nine percent perspiration."

Emotional Arc

Select a traditional tale that you know well or a story from your own life. On a piece of paper or in a journal write out the progression of the story. What is the beginning? What follows that? What is the end? Now make another progression, this time following the emotional arc. How do you want the listener to feel about the elements in the first progression? How do you want the listener to feel at the end of the story?

To work through those larger questions step by step, here is another set of questions to answer:

- How do you introduce the listener to the narrator and to the circumstance of the story?
- How and where do you move them along a path of identity, sympathy, like or dislike, comfort or not
- How and where do you build or release tension?
- What is the emotional climax of the story?
- How do you want the listener to feel at that moment?
- Where is the emotional climax compared to the end of story?
- What has to happen between the climax and the end?

As a variation on this exercise, try to work up two alternate versions of the story as if it were a sport with four quarters. Create one where the climax comes somewhere in the third quarter of the story and the entire last period is about coasting to success. Create another in which the climax is at the very end, just as the clock is ticking off the last seconds and success will depend on one last heroic effort. Let the tension build until the last line and then, as they say, "finish pretty."

continued on next page

Moral Framework

Select a traditional tale that you know well or a story from your own life. On a piece of paper or in a journal write out the progression of the story. What is the beginning? What follows that? What is the end? What is the moral framework of your story? Do you fundamentally approve or disapprove of what happens? Do you want the audience to approve or disapprove of the circumstances of this difficult story? What do you say and how do you say it, to make it so?

As a variation on this exercise, try crafting a story with a moral framework that you do *not* fundamentally agree with. Can you suspend your own judgment long enough to inhabit that world view? Can you see where in these circumstances someone might reasonably believe and act on those beliefs in a way that is the opposite of your approach?

Confidentiality, Community, and Practice

The only way out is through.
—Henry David Thoreau

Undertaking the work of telling difficult stories means undertaking a journey that may not go directly to a safe harbor. The Israelites wandered the desert for forty years before they entered the Promised Land. Even then, Moses did not set foot upon that soil he had left Egypt to find. When the lawyer takes up the case, there is no guarantee that the jury will agree. When the organizer goes into the community, the issues that brought him there often give way to more fundamental issues that must be solved first.

There is a lot of work to the telling of difficult stories. Work to identify what stories can be told. Work to shape them in ways that make their meanings clear. There is also the deep personal work that is necessary for the teller to be a clear conduit for the tale. You can utilize every element suggested in this volume to craft your material. If, however, you do not have emotional control over the story, all that work will be for nothing. The story is not ready to share with others until you control it, and is no longer in control of you.

Toward that end, you will want to develop ever-widening

circles of emotional safety for telling your stories. As we have said, it is unfair to listeners (and certainly to paying audiences) to tell material before it is ready, and yet the best way to develop truthful and artful stories is to tell them repeatedly to understanding listeners.

Is this a paradox? Yes, but the truth is that when a story must be told, it must also be heard. And we mean heard by you as you tell it out loud and by another who is not personally emotionally invested in the story.

To do the work of preparing difficult stories, it is necessary to find the particular person(s) you trust to whom you can tell and from whom you can receive feedback. Extreme care should be taken in choosing compadres in this early stage. The word *compadre* means "to parent with." In the Hispanic tradition, it refers to those people you trust enough to ask to be godparents to your children. The story is like a new baby. You may not yet be ready to deal with those who only want to tell you that the baby's head is pointed—or worse yet, those who insist you didn't need to have a baby in the first place. You want to surround yourself with those people you trust with the birthing experience.

This might be a friend, your significant other, your minister, or your therapist. Whoever it is, he should know that you are testing unfinished material. He should be able to listen to the story without interruption. He should be able to withhold judgment about the meaning or worth of the story in favor of inquiry. He should make note of the things he doesn't understand or ask questions to clarify what is being said and why. He should be honest in his response and gentle in his criticism. There is a real need for maintaining confidentiality in this work, both to provide a safe context for you to explore these topics and to protect the integrity of the story.

You may find that those who are closest to you are not capable of filling this need. If so, do not fault them. Often those who love us dearly have difficulty being cast in this role. They are uncomfortable with the material. They may be concerned about what we want to share with the world. Growth is often painful. Like a literal birthing process, it is not always easy to watch. This is not work for the squeamish or timid. You may need to look outside your immediate circle of family or friends to find the appropriate person(s). Sometimes another person who is equally interested in storytelling is the best choice.

After you have had the opportunity to shape the story with one trusted person, it can be tried with other individuals. Then you can move to a small group, then to ever-widening circles until you fully know and truly own the material. Why? Two essential things happen when you develop difficult story material in this way.

First, the story changes as the listener (the audience) changes. Stories grow and shift in response to who hears them. This is especially true when the same listener hears the same story more than once. They hear, and you tell, different aspects each time. As questions are posed or criticism is offered, you have the opportunity to sharpen the point or smooth out the rough edges as you choose.

Secondly, there is a value to testing your material in many different ways, with a widening circle of listeners. It is a way of building community. It is a way of building support for the artful speaking of truth. You can gauge what different listeners respond to and select those details and structures that best suit your purpose in telling the story. You can come to a sense of when is the right time to tell this story this way. You can figure out what can be told at the Rotary Club and what at church before you actually arrive at those places.

Storytelling guilds may be excellent places to share your stories. That is, however, not always the case. Some guilds are open to hearing new material of all kinds. Others are made up of individuals who have preconceived ideas about what topics are appropriate for storytelling. Even one or two people of that kind in a group can make the situation uncomfortable for the fledgling teller of the difficult tale. Far better to invite two or more like-minded individuals to work with you privately than to expose your infant story in such an unhealthy climate. Actors and writers often form small groups for intense individual work, meeting frequently over short periods of time for mutual artistic support.

No matter how you choose to structure this process, do not expect it to be sure, fast, or painless. There are times and stories about which even your closest friends do not want to hear. Or do not want to hear without some kind of protection built into the situation. At the start of this book, we said you should be kind to yourself. Do not ask of yourself that which you feel would be too demanding for someone else in your situation. You should also extend that courtesy to those who help you shape the stories you want to tell.

We also said you should not hesitate to seek help if ideas from this book bring up feelings that are too intense for you to deal with alone. We stand by that statement. The fact that you have come this far suggests that you have been careful, that you haven't run away screaming or thrown this book out the nearest window. Or if you have, you've had a chance to think it over and decided to retrieve it from the flower bed and give the process another chance.

It is our hope that it has been of some value to you. Remember: Be bold, be bold, but not too bold. Tell well, tell artfully, tell truthfully, tell often.

Difficult Stories and Spirituality

A book must be the axe for the frozen sea inside of us.

> —Kafka, letter to Oskar Pollak,
> January 27, 1904

We invited a number of people to make annotated recommendations about books that they found especially helpful in thinking about storytelling, spirituality, and difficult stories. Here is a sampling of what came back to us:

Barron, Frank, Alfonso Montuori, and Anthea Barron. *Creators on Creating.* New York: Jeremy P. Tarcher/Putnam, 1997.

> A collection of essays, interviews, and reflections on the creative process with artists of all stripes. It includes the Federico Fellini quote that I believe is a wonderful statement of my approach to storytelling: "I have invented myself entirely, a childhood, a personality, longings, memories and dreams, all in order to be able to tell them." —LN

Calbow, Lorraine Lum. *This Little Light of Mine: Remembering the Light Within.* Tempe, Ariz.: (self-published) Light of Mine Press (P.O. Box 23930, Tempe, AZ 85285), 2000.

> A thoughtful reflection on what it means to follow a spirit l path using the material of self. —LN

Campbell, Joseph. *The Hero with a Thousand Faces*. Princeton: Princeton University Press, 1949.

At some point, you have to read the classics, and this is a primal text on mythmaking. His style is wide ranging, eclectic, and in laying out the argument for the journey of the hero, Campbell provides plenty of material for thinking about why and how we tell these stories.   —LN

Dillard, Annie. *For the Time Being*. New York: Vintage Books, 1999.

She deals with all the big issues of life, death, and meaning and does it in a very compelling way. I find myself reflecting on the images she created and the ideas she evoked. —Nan Kammann

Eliach, Yaffa. *Hasidic Tales of the Holocaust*. New York: Oxford University Press, 1982.

A unique collection of oral histories which reveal the difference between spiritual and physical survival and give historical significance to dreams, visions, and visitations.   —Gerald Fierst

Gaskin, Stephen. *Sunday Morning Services on the Farm*. Vol. 1. Summertown, Tenn.: The Book Publishing Company, n.d.

It's just what it says, transcripts of Gaskin's sermons from the mid-1970s, the heyday of The Farm. This is hard to find, but I not only would not sell it, I would run into a burning house to save it.   —Deb Keefer

Gersie, Alida. *Earth Tales*. London: Green Print, 1992.

And she has another one that I haven't been able to get hold of yet: *Storymaking in Bereavement*. I took a workshop with her years ago. She's phenomenal. She is a drama therapist who uses storytelling also to empower and heal communities of low income, high crime that she works with in England.   —Noa Baum

Hillman, James. *The Soul's Code*. New York: Random House, 1999.

Currently the smartest man in the world, in my opinion, James Hillman re-imagines psychology as an aesthetic art form, not merely a chemical or behavioral science. He places character at the center of a life and "reads" a personality backwards according to

its "acorn" or "Daimon." Each life is a novel. Fun to re , too,
he illustrates his ideas through famous personalities.

—Mega Wells

Hillman, James. *Kinds of Power: A Guide to its Intelligent Us* New
York: Doubleday, 1998.

Again, this amazingly smart guy plays with psychologica nages
of power from an aesthetic literary point of view.

—Mega Wells

Horwitz, Claudia. *A Stone's Throw: Living the Act of Faith, Social
Transformation through Faith and Spiritual Practice*. Durham,
N.C.: Stone Circles, 1999.

A wonderful book that's actually a field guide to social change and
spiritual practice. Not only full of wonderful stories and inspi-
rational anecdotes but lots of great exercises, activities, meditations, and rituals. I would take this book with me if I were on a
desert island and had only a few choice items to take with me.

—Diane Johnson

Kurtz, Ernest. *The Spirituality of Imperfection: Modern Wisdom from
Classic Stories*. New York: Bantam Books, 1992.

A kind of buffet table for those who want a lot of rich morsels to
choose from but want them in smaller digestible portions. —LN

Martin, Calvin Luther. *The Way of the Human Being*. New Haven
Conn.: Yale University Press, 1999.

From the introduction: "Native America has always posed a
challenge to western civilization. The challenge cuts deeply, deeper
than we generally care to go: it asks us to examine the fundamental
nature of knowledge and even reality itself." Even if you do not
tell Native American stories, Martin's elegant and honest book
enlarges our view of the indigenous world. —Carol Birch

Maxwell, William. *Billie Dyer and Other Stories*. New York: Alfred
A. Knopf, 1992.

The longtime beloved fiction editor of *The New Yorker*, writer of
stories and novels, tells the stories he is most ashamed of and talks
about why he has to tell them. —Nancy Duncan

May, Rollo. *The Cry for Myth.* New York: Norton, 1991.

Like the wooden framing of a house, myths/stories support cultural beliefs, becoming the narratives by which we relate our inner selves to the outside world. Eloquent language, provocative ideas, and a celebration of Story's pre-eminence. —Carol Birch

Meade, Erika Helm. *Tell It By Heart: Women and the Healing Power of Story.* Chicago: Open Court Publishing Company, 1995.

A storyteller and a therapist, Meade has written a warm, funny, affecting, and accessible book of case studies that show how various folktales and cultural myths have been used to reflect and illuminate the lives of her clients. I bought it as an impulse buy with birthday money because I liked the cover, and it has become one of the books that I give away most often as gifts.

—Nancy Donoval

Meade, Michael. *Men and the Water of Life: Initiating and the Tempering of Men.* San Francisco: HarperSanFrancisco, 1993.

Michael believes that the place of our deepest wound is the place where, upon re-visitation, we find our most important life's work. If men took their internal life as seriously as women, this would have sold like *Women Who Run with the Wolves.* It has that kind of power to change lives. —Jim May

Needleman, Jacob. *Money and the Meaning of Life.* New York: Doubleday, 1991.

This is a very spiritual book, so your first thought might be that its message is that we attach too much importance to money. In fact, Needleman argues that money is sacred and powerful and that what the material society does is to trivialize money, and that that is the root of our schizophrenic relationship to wealth, class, and work. Also narrated through a story format. —Deb Keefer

Newman, Leslea. *A Letter to Harvey Milk.* Ithaca, New York: Firebrand Books, 1988.

A collection of short stories by one of America's leading feminist, Jewish, gay writers. The nature of sexuality is often taken for granted within the emotional universe of the characters who come to life in these tales as people who seek love, connection, and continuity. —Gerald Fierst

Pearson, Carol S. *The Hero Within: Six Archetypes We Live By.* New York: HarperSanFrancisco/HarperCollins, 1989.

Pearson explores six types of heroes and the journeys they travel: Innocent, Orphan, Wanderer, Martyr, Warrior, Magician. She looks at the way we cycle through these versions of the protagonist in our own lives, what tasks we must do, what lessons we need to learn, and some consequences if we get stuck too long in one role. She pays particular attention to how women often move through these archetypes differently than men, as she feels that has been a bit neglected in other hero journey explorations. —Nancy Donoval

Portelli, Alessandro. *The Death of Luigi Trastulli and Other Stories.* Albany: State University of New York Press, 1991.

A wonderful book on the process of how we move from personal experience to the "practiced" narrative. Though ostensibly about the collection and use of oral histories, it speaks directly to the human need to organize chaos as story. —LN

Some, Maidoma Patrice. *Of Water and Spirit: Ritual, Ma[illegible], and Initiation in the Life of an African Shaman.* New York: [illegible]kana-Penguin, 1995.

A fascinating look into the culture of a thoroughly wes[illegible]nized African man (with two Ph.D.s) who also swims in the [illegible]cient cosmological waters of the West African Dagara peop[illegible], who believe that pain opens us to the spirit world. —J[illegible] May

Stroup, Karen, Linda Quigley, Carol Osborn, and Susan [illegible]uner. *Speak the Language of Healing: How to Have Breast Cancer [illegible]ithout Going to War.* Berkeley: Conari Press, 1999.

Four women from Nashville, each with different stages of breast cancer and from four different religious viewpoints, tell their stories of each of five stages of treatment—powerfully honest material. —Nancy Duncan

Thorne, Julia with Larry Rothstein. *You Are Not Alone.* New York: HarperCollins Publishers. 1993.

Julia Thorne combines her own story with moving first-person accounts of experiences of depression and recovery, offering individuals and their families empathy, information, spiritual and emotional awareness, and companionship.

—Dorothy Cleveland

Windling, Terri, ed. *The Armless Maiden and Other Tales for Childhood's Survivors.* New York: Tor Books, 1995.

The Armless Maiden is a book that speaks straight to the bone and marrow of many dark and difficult stories. Filled with stories and poems that mine fairy-tale metaphors to explore, perhaps understand, certainly give voice to childhood abuses, it is Windling's own Afterword that I find most moving. Listed as an essay, it is an exquisitely written personal narrative detailing a visit home during a family crisis in which she and her brother finally exchange their truths about their childhood. As she puts it, "Fairy tales were a kind of magic that protected me as a child. Not my body, bruised and battered, they protected my spirit and kept it alive . . . Fairy tales were not my escape from reality as a child; rather, they were my reality—for mine was a world in which good and evil were not abstract concepts. Like fairy-tale heroines, no magic could save me unless I had the wit and heart and courage to use it wisely."

—Nancy Donoval

Zinsser, William. *Inventing the Truth: The Art and Craft of Memoir.* Boston: Houghton Mifflin Company, 1987.

A collection of memoirs by Russell Baker, Annie Dillard, Alfred Kazin, Toni Morrison and Lewis Thomas. My favorite lines come from Russell Baker's essay, "Life With Mother": "But he wasn't really a liar; he just wanted life to be more interesting than it was . . . Uncle Harold had perceived that the possibilities of achieving art lie not in reporting, but in fiction."   —Dorothy Cleveland